Around Ireland Clockwise on a "Giant".

For Mr. Jack Brewer, who was my mentor and a source of inspiration for me throughout my career.

by

Patrick McEvoy.

Patrick McEvoy.

Sept. 2011.

www.AroundIrelandClockWiseOnAGiant.com

First Paperback Edition.

ISBN-13:
978-1907659034

(APOLLO PUBLISHING)

ISBN-10:
190765903X

Acknowledgements.

I am so grateful for all the support of not only my family but all those wonderful people who supported me in so many different ways throughout my journey. They made it not only fun but a most enjoyable, interesting and exciting experience which I hope to be able to repeat when I get to eighty years of age, except that I'll then do it anti clockwise in the height of summer and perhaps use a cycle fitted with battery assistance!

Patrick McEvoy.

That place was all UPHILL!

Introduction:

This trip around the coastline of Ireland came to mind when I retired at the age of sixty years. What I had in mind then was to walk around the whole coastline but advice from various sources at that time persuaded me to temporarily abandon the idea. From then until my approaching seventieth birthday in 2009 I kept turning the idea over in my mind. However, instead of walking the whole way I decided that perhaps it would be a better idea to cycle the coastline as this would avoid me having to carry a heavy rucksack. I could put my tent etc., on the cycle. The only part of this idea which troubled me was that just prior to my sixtieth birthday I had cycled in northern France for two weeks. In those two weeks my backside, legs and wrists took such a hammering on the rough side roads of Brittany that I vowed never to do such a silly thing again as to ride a cycle other than for maybe an hour or two at any one time. Another factor which concerned me was that of health. In 1991 I had a triple heart bypass but, fortunately not a heart attack. The result of that operation made me feel even more fit than before. However, during the end of a four year period of continuing world travel, mainly in a motor home, I was in Canada when I suffered a heart attack. I came back to the UK to recover but the wanderlust was still in my system and so I decided that no matter what, I would attempt to cycle around the whole of the coastline of Ireland to celebrate my seventieth birthday in April, 2009. With cautious advice from my doctor I began to make plans as to what cycle and equipment I would need. Whether to cycle in a clockwise or anti clockwise direction was, I was told, another important factor. Furthermore, I had never slept in a tent in my life let alone know what sort of tent to choose. And so preparations began on all fronts.

In the week before Christmas 2008, with a tent which I was certain would suit my Ireland expedition exactly, I went to a camp site on the Spanish Mediterranean for twenty one days to try out not only the tent but to sample life under canvas for the first time. There were two nights of gale force winds but I was in a very sheltered corner of the camp-site and everything was o.k. It also rained on a few of the days but the tent withstood that too. The tent I had chosen was one in which I could stand up and had a large two-zip door which could be lifted upwards to accommodate the rear of a five door car. It didn't seem particularly heavy to me at 7.5 kilos and neither did it seem too bulky. I came back full of confidence in the preparations I was making for my adventure in Ireland.4. A month or two before going to Spain with the tent I had bought an almost new 'Giant' make pedal cycle, model 'Expression DX W' from a well-known cycle shop in Goole. I then rode it daily to try and avoid a repeat experience of my cycling trip to France. I had it fitted it out with everything I could possibly need plus all necessary equipment to meet most eventualities such as punctures, chain and gear malfunctions, if any, and of course the most comfortable seat possible. It transpired that I could not have chosen a more suitable bicycle for the task. I also made sure I had appropriate clothing as advised in all of the numerous books I had read on the subject, not only of cycling but of cycling in Ireland. There was only one snag with all of the cycling books I read. None of them related to anyone, of any age, who had cycled around the whole of Ireland's coastline in one continuous period. All related to cycling up and down and across and one or two covered cycling around some of the coastal areas of Ireland in periods of a month or so at a time. All of the authors had rarely spent any time in a tent having preferred to stay in B&BS etc. and most were accompanied by either another adult or partner. Nevertheless I learnt lots of useful information from their observations and experience which I hoped would help me in my venture.

I had planned to do the trip in an anti-clockwise direction on the grounds that if I started off somewhere on the northern coast and travelled westward then southward along the west coast I would be attacking the greatest mountains and hills when I would be at my strongest. From maps, plus some earlier visits to Ireland in a vehicle in previous years, I knew that the greatest concentration of coastal hills and mountains was on those two coastlines. However, the greatest deciding factor was to be wind direction. I knew an expert on the prevailing winds around most of the world. His expertise came from advising companies building wind turbines. He advised me to travel clockwise around Ireland to get the most benefit from the prevailing westerly winds from the Atlantic. The one thing I disliked most from my teenage experience of cycling in the north of Ireland was that of cycling into a strong headwind. Therefore I abandoned the plan of cycling in an anti-clockwise direction in favour of the clockwise direction. One of the books I had read estimated the coastal route along main roads to be in the region of 2000 miles. As I intended travelling all the roads around the coastline, keeping as close as possible to the sea, this information didn't help so I resorted to some of the Internet's most famous search engines. One stated that the Ordnance Survey distance of the coastline was 1,970.5 miles. Another gave the figure of the coastline as 4660 miles (7,500 km) and yet another stated that the coastline measured 2,300 miles (3,700km). As these distances related to the coastline and not the coast roads I reckoned on the total road distance to be somewhere about 2000 miles.

Eric Newby in his excellent book "Round Ireland in Low Gear" stated that the coastline of Ireland was 3,500 miles long. Peninsulas such as the Iveragh, the Beara and the Dingle Head Peninsulas are between thirty and forty miles long. To skirt the perimeter of these four adjacent peninsulas would involve a journey of at least 255 miles. The Ring of Kerry on the Iveragh Peninsula alone is over 100 miles and at the end of it one would only be about sixty miles further along on one's way. Similar vast detours would also have to be made, if one was serious about it, all the way up the West coast.

This aspect of the trip didn't worry me too much as I planned to set off about the end of April or early May and I felt sure that I could cover the whole route before the end of August or early September. Anyway, I was satisfied that that by the end of the trip I would have the exact distance in miles / kilometres as I had purchased a milometer employing the latest computerised technology. It not only calculated distances travelled but average and actual speeds travelled and even the length of times stopped.

This trip was not to be about how long it would take me to do it or how fast I had travelled. I was going to take my time and enjoy the experience. It was not to be about visiting places of historical significance or any other specification. If anything I was looking forward to meeting people along the way and gaining experience of long distance cycling around the country of my birth. A third but not vital quest was that of health. I had had a heart bypass operation in 1991 and a heart attack in 2002 so I wondered how my heart would stand up to the obvious strain put upon it. On one point I was determined however. It was that wherever possible I would cycle every continuous coast road all the way round the coastline. By that I mean that I would not go on one-way roads out to the ends of peninsulas for example and then have to ride back along the same road. From my maps I saw that many of the coastal roads were also main roads but I set my mind on following all the roads closest to the sea. The solution I was going to adopt, as far as directions were concerned, was simply to keep the sea on my left hand side at all times. I needed no fancy GPS system! For my 70th birthday in April my family had bought me an IPhone. They made special mention of its in-built GPS function and were maybe a little disappointed when I said jokingly, "Oh I won't need that to guide me. For directions all I need to do is keep the sea always on my left hand side". But of course I used it practically every day.

Patrick McEvoy.

The Adventure.

On Wednesday, 28th April 2009 I arrived at Belfast City Airport on an early morning flight from Robin Hood Airport in the UK. My bike was duly unloaded from the 'plane. I had packed it as required with the front wheel removed and secured against the frame. Hardboard protected both sides of the rather large package. I had used strong rope, similar to a clothes line, to secure everything in place and provided adequate handles for flight staff to hold and carry the bike upright. I was therefore a bit perturbed when I saw it being carried horizontally by the two goods staff. Neither of the men were holding the handles I had provided for the carrying of the bike. Sure enough when I unpacked it the rear wheel was very badly buckled. The damage was so bad that to enable the wobbling wheel to turn I had to totally remove the whole brake unit on the rear wheel. However, I was so relieved that my packaging had prevented any damage to the cycle's 21 gear mechanism.

I realised that before I could think about setting out on my trip I would have to get the bike to a repair shop and await its repair, which would delay me for at least a day or more. There I was in the Airport Arrivals, with passengers going to and fro, trying to get everything together and onto the bike. Somehow the flight's Public Relations Officer became aware that I was having some

difficulty and arrived at my side. She introduced herself
as Moira and in a most caring and helpful manner asked
me if I was having some sort of problem. I explained
what had happened. She apologised on behalf of the
company involved and offered whatever help she could
give. She explained the procedure for claiming for the
damage caused but all I wanted to get sorted at that
stage was the wheel to be repaired. However, on advice
from Moira I decided that as a precaution I should get
booked into overnight accommodation in the city until
the cycle problem was resolved. She brought me a most
welcome cup of tea and said I could take whatever
length of time I needed to get everything sorted out
where I was. Having removed the rear brake unit I
decided that I could load everything onto the bike and
then slowly and carefully ride it into town to a repair
shop. Moira returned with details of a Guest House in
the city and informed me that there was a big cycle
repair shop very close to it. I went with her to the Travel
Desk and accepted the offer of the Guest House and was
assured that there was secure storage there for my bike.

My next problem was the weight of the four panniers,
the tent, the tarpaulin, my rucksack and myself was such
that there was no way I could even attempt to ride the
bike anywhere let alone out into the busy streets of
Belfast to look for a cycle repair shop. There was the
risk that the wheel would simply collapse altogether.
The big mistake I had made at home was that I foolishly
hadn't loaded the four fully laden panniers, plus my tent
and a fairly large tarpaulin onto the cycle and go for a
test ride. With my weight at 13 stone; the cycle at 3

stone and the combined weight of the tent and the four pannier totally at least another 4 stone totalled a staggering 20 stone! I couldn't believe what I had done. At home I had only thought of the weight of the panniers and the tent and ignored the total weight involved.

I had by now put my tent to one side, plus several other items I felt I could well manage without until I had the wheel repaired viz. (spare tyre; rucksack and sleeping bag plus various items of clothing and the tarpaulin) all of which reduced at least the overall bulk involved. Again Moira came to my rescue by suggesting that if I wanted I could borrow a smaller but brand new unused tent which she had at home and she would keep my much bigger and bulkier tent, plus any other unwanted items, until I had completed my trip around Ireland. But I would have to return the following day to the airport to collect her tent. I readily agreed.

An hour or so later I wheeled my now much lighter and less bulky outfit into the street and very carefully set off for the Marantha Guest House at 254 Ravenhill Road, in the city. Before I set off I made a very slow and steady test ride around the airport forecourt watched by Moira. She was quite clearly worried that I wouldn't make it to the Guest House safely. The wheel was so badly buckled that as I rode off I could feel the extreme wobbling of the rear end of the cycle. It was as if I was on one of those fancy machines in a gym which gyrates the lower body to help lose weight.

I lost my way twice but got detailed guidance first from a group of young women and then from a young man in the street. His direction was all I needed but somehow I passed the same group of young women who had earlier given me the directions. They gave me a big cheer and asked if they could have a ride, etc. I must have looked a sight with my wobbling rear end and all my bright red and yellow clothing and helmet but their jovial manner and sense of fun cheered me up.

Eventually I arrived at the guest house. It had a big open space in front to park several cars. I didn't see anywhere for my bike to be out of sight and secure like they told me at the airport Travel Office. I temporarily locked it to the fence and rang the doorbell. The proprietor's mother, Mrs Ann Bree, made me very welcome from the moment she opened the door. The first thing I mentioned was my apprehension about my bike. "Don't you worry Patrick. We'll see that you bike is totally secure overnight. But first, come and see that your room is what you would like. We were told that you had a lot of stuff on your bike so we've put you in a big room on the ground floor to save you carrying it up the stairs". The room was perfect in every respect. After I had removed the panniers and other items from the bike and put them in my room she said "Now, let's get your bike sorted". She called her son, Dennis (the proprietor), a hefty young man of about 25, and took me into their large and luxurious sitting room. They pulled the big leather settee away from the wall and told me that was where my bike was going to be put overnight. I felt a bit guilty at seeing what they had done to reassure me.

Probably my bike would have been quite safe where it was for one night.

After a very welcome meal I walked up the Ravenhill Road to check out the location of the bike shop. It wasn't far away. By that time of course it was closed. The sign read, 'Bike Dock, 79 to 85, Ravenhill Road'. Contented I headed back to 'Marantha'. During the process of booking in I told Mrs Bree about Miora having kindly volunteered to hold any of my stuff I felt I didn't need until my return whereupon she said that she too would do the same for me. So, once back in my room I emptied out everything and worked my way through it, putting to one side everything what I thought was non-essential. It was enough to fill one large black plastic refuse sack. I repacked the panniers and got to bed. As I settled down I imagined that this would be my last night in a proper bed until I reached my family in Mourne in about a week's time. I felt quite excited about the journey I was going to undertake. Despite this set back with the buckled wheel I felt sure that my trip would be an exciting one, full of interest and fun. The wonderful help I had had at the airport from Moira and the welcome by Mrs Bree was setting the tone, I was sure, for the rest of the trip. The following morning I was treated to what Mrs Bree called a 'Belfast Breakfast'. Everything by way of meat and vegetables which could be fried was on that plate. I certainly felt sure I would not get another fry-up like this anywhere else on my trip.

By 9.30 I was at 'Bike Dock' with my bike. The proprietor, Derek Armstrong, when he heard of my plight instructed the mechanic to take my bike into the workshop and treat its repair as a priority. "Come back in about half an hour" he said, "and we'll have it ready for you". I couldn't believe what I was hearing. I fully expected, at best, that it wouldn't be ready until that afternoon. I went for a look in some nearby shop windows and went back about forty minutes later only to find my bike on its stand, the wheel repaired and the mechanic busy working on another bike! I was amazed at how quickly it had been repaired. My second surprise was how little I was to be charged but Derek insisted it was all part of their customer service. As part of my load shedding exercise I offered to Derek a spare tyre which I had to do with as he pleased. He said he would keep it safe for me until my return even though I insisted he sell it. I replaced the spare tyre with a high pressure tyre inflator which was also a puncture repair system.

I sped back to the guest house, booked in for a second night then headed off to see Moira at the airport. She produced the tent she had told me about. I didn't open it up but could see its size and dimensions on its case. It was only half the weight of my tent and its size wasn't much bigger than a large loaf of bread. She had brought back everything I had given her the day before in case I wanted to change my mind about any of it. I only took back my sleeping bag and the tarpaulin. We had a coffee together and then I was on my way up to the north coast so that I could officially start my trip. I had already decided that I would begin it there at the famous Giant's

Causeway.

I chose this starting point because of the word 'Giant' being not only in the name of the location but also being the make of my bike. In what seemed like no time I was out in the open countryside on this lovely warm spring morning with the sun blazing down to my right from a clear blue sky. I was so happy. I was now going to face a challenge which I had set myself and I was looking forward to enjoying it and its successful conclusion approximately 2000 miles away. My bike simply glided along. I played with the 21 gears now that I was fully laden. Hills came and went without any great effort on my part as the gears seen to that side of things. The milometer was silently calculating all sorts of statistics and the only real sound was the whirring of the tyres on the smooth dry tarmac. At Glengormley I took the B59 which I followed towards Ballymena until I came to the junction signposted to Moorfields. This I reckoned would keep me away from any involvement with the traffic laden A26 further northwards. After Moorfields I rode a short distance on the very busy A36 which was laden with large lorries and vans no doubt heading and from the port of Larne. I deduced this from the many English and foreign registration plates and company names on the vehicles. Their size, or rather my small size by comparison, was something that I didn't really relish but I knew I would just have to get used to it somehow. Had it been dark or raining or there being any fog I wouldn't have dared risk my life on any such road. But today was different and I was such a happy bunny as I rode along in my bright red fluorescent clothing plus the red, ex Royal Mail, panniers with their fluorescent flashes. Further on I joined the B94 which would keep me going in an almost straight line for the Giants Causeway. I took little notice of anything other than the road ahead, the milometer reading and the odd quick glance at the map. Broughshane came and went as did Clogh, then Ballymoney. In the town I took a sharp right onto the B66 up to Dervock following the signs to Bushmills; the town which gave its name to that brand of whiskey known worldwide. As much as I would have liked 'a wee nip of the hard stuff ' I dared not dally as I had a long hard ride ahead of me along the hilly coast road back to Belfast. It was now lunchtime and I was already thinking that I had bitten off more than I could chew, as the saying goes, on this my very first day on the pedals.

I arrived at the entrance leading to the Giant's Causeway car park and complex at 1.20 pm. This was my starting off point. A few buses were disgorging their passengers, cars were coming and going. I paused for a few moments and tried to imagine my feelings as I would once again cycle up to this spot having completed the circuit of the country. With those thoughts in mind I got the pedals turning and was on my way towards Ballintoy. Not very far along the road I saw the sign that Benbane Head was over on my left. Behind me, to the west, thick clouds were forming promising a very colourful sunset. By then I hoped I would be in or very near Belfast. In what seemed no time at all I was past Ballintoy village and flying along towards Ballycastle. I passed several small groups of rucksack laden walkers, mainly young men and women. They were walking two and sometimes three abreast on this rather narrow twisty road. Several times I had to use my bell to warn them of my approach but not one took my action to be one of anything but care for them. I got a cheery wave from most of them and a few shouts in a foreign language. Labels on their rucksacks indicated they were Swedish. Again I would have liked to ride beside some of them and talk about their country which I love so much but I felt time pressing me onwards. It did occur to me that maybe I should forget about getting back to Belfast that evening and perhaps find a hostel or B & B to stay in overnight. The hills in this direction were short and steep in places with long gentle downhill slopes away ahead. At times my free-wheeling speed on these downhill slopes scared me. In places I was sure I was doing about thirty miles per hour but it was lovely to just sit back and let the Giant go. Rabbits were continually dashing across in front of me. One came half way across then stopped and turned back. I thought I was going to hit it but missed it by inches. If I had hit it I might have suffered more than the rabbit.

Approaching Ballycastle I saw land about five miles off shore. At first I thought it was the Mull of Kintyre in Scotland but no it was Rathlin Island which my map duly confirmed. I stopped a while, had a refreshing drink and had a closer look with my binoculars but couldn't make out anything except hills. Two motorcyclists stopped and asked if they could look at my map. They were from France I think and were heading for Derry to re-join another party of

motorcyclists travelling from Belfast. They very kindly
handed me back my map accompanied by a fairly large
box of chocolates before roaring off up the road on their
massive machines. I made those chocolates last me two
days. What a nice gesture from them! In Ballycastle I
stopped near the harbour wall for about twenty minutes
to have a sandwich and was immediately joined by a
lone seagull which made it quite clear to me that it
expected a sample of my sandwich. I made it wait on
half the crust before letting it have it. No sooner had the
gull snapped it up than about half a dozen more
descended on it, all within about three feet or so from
me. A fierce squabble ensued with even more joining in.
Eventually the first one managed to fly off only with
half of the piece I had thrown. The remaining gulls
surrounded me expectantly but I had nothing left for
them. I certainly wasn't going to part with one of my
chocolates! However, the whole scene changed
dramatically when a man on what was obviously a small
fishing boat in the harbour, began throwing the contents
of a bucket into the water. I assumed it was the remains
of fish caught earlier. In a flash the seagulls around me
were gone in that direction but not before a few hundred
gulls descended on the boat from all directions
screeching something terrible. If they had done that to
me I think I would have let them have my precious
chocolates and made a run for it! When I rode off later
the action was in full swing. It was to be the only
excitement I was to witness that afternoon as I pedalled
furiously southwards. About a mile outside Ballycastle I
headed off down what I hoped was a through road
signposted Loughran and Runaboy head. There was no
life to be seen except wildlife in the form of endless

flocks of swirling seagulls out over the sea and at one point about twenty or more geese flying southwards in their typical V formation. Had they too had enough of the seagulls I wondered? A sign showing Cushendun ahead reassured me that this wasn't a one way road as my map showed me it was on the A2.

From there to Larne the map showed hardly any land between the road and the sea and that was what in most cases it turned out to be with high cliffs on my left overlooking the sea most of the way. The view was spectacular both out over the sea and up to the high mountain tops on my left where I could see lots of sheep grazing peacefully and lambs playing. One quick light shower of rain came over the mountains but was soon gone out over the sea. From Glenarm onwards I kept seeing passenger steamers heading both north and southwards. No doubt they were from either Larne or Belfast or quite possibly from Scottish or English ports. I used my binoculars but the steamers were just that bit too far away to make out their names. The Antrim Mountains loomed above me on my right all the way down to Larne. In Larne I stopped at a cafe and had a quick meal. The place was very busy. All round me I recognised accents from all over England and Scotland and some from the south and west of Ireland all mingled in with foreign accents none of which I recognised.

Now it was getting dusk. I was feeling a little tired. It was only as I rode along earlier in the afternoon that I thought about how I would cope without my usual afternoon siesta to which I had become accustomed since my retirement. I couldn't just set up my tent in the mid afternoon to have my nap. Neither could I simply park my bike and lie down in the grass at the roadside as someone might get alarmed and call an ambulance or the police to investigate this man lain at the side of his bike possibly dead or ill. It looked like this was one of life's pleasures which I might have to forgo during the trip. All sorts of wild and unlikely scenarios went through my mind but kept me occupied as I cycled along mile after mile. I saw beautifully kept farmhouses both near the roadside and farther afield. The roadside in places were alight with early daffodils just coming into full bloom. Everywhere hedges in fields and on the farms were well trimmed and farm gates and barn doors all newly painted. In only a few places did I see apparently abandoned farm machinery plus here and there an isolated caravan parked in a field. I noticed this air of tidiness since setting off this morning from Belfast.

As I made my way through Larne the whole cycling experience changed. The sunset I anticipated never materialised. Instead the sky had darkened and a steady drizzle of rain began. I had no option but to follow the main road through Glynn village and keep along what I took to be the coast road to Whitehead. It was in fact the road along Larne Lough. In the gathering dusk I missed the significance of taking the B150 onto Magee Island. It would have been a round trip of perhaps eight or nine miles but would have given me a welcome break from the constant heavy traffic of huge lorries and vans obviously coming from or going to the ports of Larne or Belfast. At times they were quite slow moving which meant that I was just a matter of a few feet from their huge wheels. Large protruding wing mirrors on most of them were at times only a matter of perhaps a foot from my shoulder. Wherever possible I rode along slowly on my nearside footpath. I saw other cyclists doing the same. This was something I had not anticipated. Another hazard that evening, but one experienced many times later throughout my trip, was puddles of water near the kerb edge. Often they concealed potholes of various depths and even blocked drains. I couldn't move outwards to avoid the water otherwise I would be in the path of the traffic so at each puddle, and there were a lot, I really slowed down and eased my way through them carefully. Riding on the footpath was the best, although illegal, solution.

From Whitehead on to Belfast via Carrickfergus, Glengormley, the situation remained almost the same except for when the dual carriageway and motorway intervened. All the way along the Belfast Lough I could clearly see the street lights of Bangor and Hollywood. They were reflected in the smooth waters of the Lough. I would have liked to have been able to stop and admire the scene, even photograph it, but my personal safety was slightly more on my mind as I worked my way steadily towards Maranatha Guest House and my supper. Mrs Bree very kindly made me a sumptuous meal. Once again my bike, dripping with rain, got parked behind the settee. This time however, I had insisted on putting some newspapers under it but I didn't feel happy about the inconvenience they were putting on themselves.

The milometer showed that I had travelled 97 miles since setting out in the morning. I promised myself not to undertake another trek like that in the future. After a most welcome hot bath I erected Moira's tent in my room and tried it out for size. I was pleasantly surprised at the space I had in it. It was big enough for me to sleep fully stretched out plus my four panniers and rucksack along one side with some space along the other side. Height wise it was ok. I could even kneel upright in it. Now fully relaxed and happy I went to sleep like a little schoolboy on his first holiday.

The following morning I woke from a strange dream, or maybe nightmare, about being chased along a road on my bike by a lorry laden down with screeching seagulls which were also in the cab encouraging the driver to get me! My only escape was to go over the cliff edge but I kept going as fast as I could and somehow avoided them. I hoped it wasn't some sort of omen for the future.

After another of Mrs Bree's 'Belfast Breakfasts' I was ready for take off from Maranatha Guest House and the care of Mrs Bree. By then all four panniers were properly secured, my waterproof clothing and tarpaulin were on the front carrier with my rucksack and tent on the rear carrier. I made sure the weight on the front was not too much as to affect my steering so the lighter items were concentrated there. Farewells done I set off up the Ravenhill Road to an O2 shop get my two mobile phones topped up and adjusted so that I could use them throughout Ireland. Now I was all set for off, or so I thought. My first destination was Hollywood. I had gone about a mile when I realised that my milometer was not functioning. I stopped, checked its setting and connection but everything seemed OK. I got out the instructions and read them, especially the troubleshooting section but still no answer. There was only one answer; go to Bike Dock. That didn't take long but when I got there several customers were waiting for attention. I managed a quick word with the mechanic I saw the other day and he had a quick look at the milometer. He couldn't see any reason why it wouldn't work and suggested that some sort of fault had obviously developed since yesterday. Another suggestion was to fit a cable type milometer. I decided that the milometer was not a necessity after all, thanked the mechanic and once more set off towards Hollywood.

By comparison with the previous day it felt quite strange riding with all this weight. How different it was from yesterday when I didn't have the panniers and the rest of the things. However, it seemed so much lighter than when I first attempted to ride it at the airport. The city traffic was no problem and soon I was almost into Hollywood. I say almost because I saw a sign to Hollywood seafront / promenade and turned left there. There were very few people on the promenade. How wonderful to have all this space to ride along in comparison to the previous evenings experience with the lorries. That memory would stay with me a long time I felt. The sun was shining, not a cloud in the sky and not even a hint of a breeze. Like the previous day the passenger steamers were busy in the Lough. I could see two in the distance. Both heading out to sea and one much closer coming in. Then a passenger 'plane appeared obviously making its way to George Best / Belfast City Airport. Everything seemed to be moving at a very slow leisurely pace; the steamers, the plane and the few people strolling along the promenade. I decided that I too would slow down; not that I was pedalling furiously or anything like that. It was time for a break, to study my map and decide on a possible overnight stopping destination. I wanted it to be a camp-site no matter what. To get into that tent and see what it would be like on my first night was something I was really looking forward to. I figured on getting on a camp-site somewhere near Bangor well before dark. I got out the five thick brochures I had picked up at the airport only to discover that they all related to accommodation at hostels. No mention of camp-sites anywhere. It didn't really worry me at that stage. I assumed that when I got near Bangor someone would know of one. Maybe I just might risk 'roughing' it some place.

Possibility of another new experience perhaps! As I was pondering on all this I saw an elderly man walking in my direction at a very brisk pace. He was swinging his arms in almost military style, head and shoulders back and quite lengthy stride. What a contrast between him and the two middle aged couples strolling along in the opposite direction. This man meant business, I could see that alright. I sat back down by my bike and watched him approaching. "Good morning" I said as he drew near. "And good morning to you too" he said in a very clear local accent and stopped in front of me. "Your bike hasn't broken down or anything?" he queried. I replied that that the bike was OK and that I had stopped for a quick break to look up some details about camp-sites near Bangor. "Why are you wearing all those clothes on a lovely warm morning like this?" was his next question. It crossed my mind that perhaps he thought I had been sleeping rough overnight and was just getting to grips with today. I felt that he was ready for a chat so I moved my bike away from the bench and made space for him to sit down and join me. I told him my name, mentioned my age and that this was my second day on my cycle trip around the whole coastline of Ireland. He congratulated me on my ambition and then asked me if I could guess his age. I honestly estimated that he was about sixty five years old. "Well thank you" he said. "Actually I am eighty years old". His name, he said, was Stanley Anderson and that he lived a short way back along the Promenade in the direction from which he had just come. We swapped our life stories and both commiserated about being widowed but I must say he was more interested in what I was intending to do than speak of his own life and his achievements. He did mention having worked in England for many years as a representative but that he liked living here in Hollywood. When I commented on his obvious high state of fitness he explained that for many years he had been a competing sprinter and had since kept up his fitness level. "I walk the full length of this promenade a good few times every day like you have just seen me doing. You can't beat good fresh air, fast walking and plenty of fruit and vegetables to eat. But most of all "he said, "It's important to eat only small meals". I was pleased that I still was wearing my baggy fluorescent jacket which prevented him from seeing my bulging waistline. Nevertheless his very presence made me sit up straight and pull in on those tummy muscles.

Eventually he stood up to go. I was about to ask if I could take his photograph when he said, "Now watch this. See if, on your way around Ireland, you meet another eighty year old man who can do this". At that he adopted a typical pose of a sprinter on the blocks waiting for the starting pistol to ring out. "Bye now" he said and before I could say another word he was gone away along the promenade at what I can only truly describe, without any exaggeration, as an amazing running speed. His arms and legs were almost a blur and from the moment he shot off he never slackened that amazing burst of speed until he was at the far end of the promenade, some three hundred yards away where it curved away out of my sight. There he stopped and waved to me then walked off just like when I had first seen him. I can honestly say I was totally amazed at what I had seen him do. Had I seen that on a film or on television I would have assumed that the film had been speeded up. I was sure I would never see an eighty year old man repeat that performance any time in my future life never mind during the trip ahead of me. In my case I wondered if, when I was eighty years of age, I could do this trip again. Maybe I could get Stanley to do it with me? But would I be able to keep up with him?

Once again I set off along the promenade towards
Hollywood but after a short distance I stopped to look at
an archway leading off the promenade on my right
leading towards a nearby housing estate. This archway
was just one big work of art. When I first saw if from a
distance I imagined I was going to witness some awful
example of vulgar graffiti. What a surprise I got as I
drew level with it and stopped to admire it. A passing
local man informed me that the previous year it had
been painted by several local teenagers who, instead of
doing graffiti there, had created this scene. It depicted
some abstracts, local scenes and even verses of poetry
all of which were painted with great care and attention
to detail. He said the paints and equipment had all been
paid for by local residents. I was impressed. He was
obviously very proud of it himself.

From where we were I could see that the promenade
ended abruptly a short distance away and asked the man
for directions to a road which would take me to Bangor.
He said I should go on ahead to the end of the
promenade then take the path across the adjacent park
from where I could follow another path back to a second
promenade and eventually onto the road to Bangor.
Within minutes I was in the park and there was the path
across it as he had described. An elderly looking lady,
bent over slightly and using a walking stick was the
only person I saw. She was walking very slowly on the
grass with her back towards me. She had a very small
dog with her on the opposite side of the path. It was not
on a lead. I was only going at a slow walking pace, very
mindful nevertheless of possibly startling the lady with

my silent approach along the smooth concrete pathway. A few yards away I gently ran the bell but didn't notice any reaction. I was ready to say a cheery "Good afternoon" to her as I passed and hoped even that wouldn't startle her too much. Suddenly as I was about level with her, my front wheel hit something rather solid and immediately a very loud howling sound began. Instinctively I stopped instantly. I knew I had hit the dog. There it was rolling over and over away from me along the path, its little short legs unable to stop its momentum until about fifteen feet away. It got to its feet and, still howling, staggered up to the lady. By this time I had got my bike on its stand and rushed to soothe the dog and hopefully pacify the lady. I fully expected that she would go berserk with me for what I had done and maybe even set about me with her walking stick. Instead she reacted so calmly. "Oh don't worry young man" she said ever so gently, "The dog is OK but you were so lucky not to have come off your bike". She picked up the dog, gave it a cuddle and a very quick inspection then set it down again. It had stopped howling but sat quietly at her feet eyeing both me and my bike with justifiable doggy alarm. I apologised profusely to her for what had happened saying that I should have been more aware of her dog than of startling her. "Stop worrying now" she said with what I recognised as a hint of authority in her voice, "and tell me what you are doing dressed like that? Are you doing something for charity?" She was by now taking in the sight of my fluorescent clothing and helmet; my bare feet in the Croc sandals and of course the bike and its bags. In as few words as possible I told her of my trip and that I was just doing it for fun to celebrate my seventieth birthday and ended by saying that this was only my second day on the road.

Well, that was the beginning of what turned out to be at least a half hour long conversation on a nearby bench, in which I learnt that she was aged 76 years, a retired head teacher at Down High School and that she was Kathleen Lindsay and that she lived locally. She was such a wonderful lady who was intent on encouraging me to persevere with my ambition almost as if I was one of her pupils. She asked if it would be the subject of a book. When I said that might be a possibility she said I was to make sure she got a copy and even offered to pay me for it in advance. I was so pleased to have made her acquaintance but obviously not in these circumstances. As we shook hands and I rode off I saw her little dog enjoying itself in some long grass nearby. What a day this was turning out to be.

At the end of the footpath I saw a much younger lady sitting on a bench holding her two dogs close to her. She was obviously aware of the earlier incident. Close to her were two large official signs clearly stating: NO CYCLING. On looking back I saw two similar signs where I had first entered the park. I stopped for a moment on the path by her and said, "I can't believe I didn't notice any of those signs". "Ah don't worry" she said, "Nobody takes any notice of them signs anyway". As we spoke she let her dogs loose and they scampered off. She told me they were both German Poodles and that one was thirteen years old and one fourteen years old". She confirmed the information from the man I had met earlier on the promenade that the narrow path nearby was the one leading to the second half of the promenade. It looked only about two feet wide with high thorn hedges overhanging from both sides. It was that narrow that I doubted if I could squeeze through it. There were also nettles and a few patches of fierce looking briars. It was too narrow to cycle through so I had to walk which made the problem worse. I headed into it hoping that my waterproofs would not get too badly damaged but I was nevertheless grateful that I had them on. It all wasn't as bad as it first appeared. I emerged virtually unscathed at the other end with no damage to my waterproofs and only a few scratches on the back of one hand. Ahead was the promenade.

Back on the promenade I again saw of Stanley Anderson striding out as before. He said he had come out for another walk as before. I took this opportunity to congratulate him on his earlier performance. "Most days I do that just to convince myself that I can still do it", he said. What a man!

In what seemed no time at all I was back on the road to Bangor but after a few miles I diverted onto a minor road. It was edging towards dusk as I rode along the Helens Bay area. The first person I saw was a woman walking a dog. She said that there might be camping up ahead in a wooded area called Crawfordsburn Park. I could see it up ahead so I rode on confidently, turning over in my mind what I would make for supper. Shortly I came to the park entrance and rode along its well-made roads following signs stating; 'Office'. The roads suddenly became so steep that I was forced to dismount and walk. In places it was so steep that I could hardly push the bike but I persevered and a eventually arrived at the office complex only to find that it was closed. To compound my annoyance there were signs everywhere stating: OVERNIGHT CAMPING STRICTLY FORBIDDEN.

I was about to leave when I spotted a car parked at the back of the office area and a light on in a nearby window. There I spoke to a man who explained that whilst he was only the cleaner he could assure me that not only was camping prohibited but that the police came up every night with a dog patrol to check if there were any campers. I set off back down the steep, very twisty park road. I had to keep the brakes on all the way down otherwise I would certainly finish up in the river overnight or maybe even longer if I wasn't found by the police!

Now I pedalled as fast as I could towards Bangor in the hope that if I didn't see any camp-site on the way then I could easily get a B & B in this, one of the most famous holiday resorts in Ireland. No camp-site materialised so next stop was the town area. Both a man in one of the main streets and a police officer in the town's police station advised me to take the road towards Donaghadee where a good many of the B & Bs were to be found. The first two where there were vacancies signs in the windows took one look at me and the bike and apologetically said they were full up. As it was now dark I held out little hope of getting anywhere to stay. For now I set my mind on finding somewhere to camp even if it was down on the beach. I could see the end of the street lights away up ahead at the top of a long hill. I felt really tired and for the moment left my quest for accommodation to fate. I saw some more VACANCIES signs but pride prevented me asking at anywhere else along the road.

At a shop I bought some milk and fruit and some very tasty sounding 'honey and yoghurt wholemeal bread'. I had never heard of that bread before but it sounded just ideal to spice up my supper and breakfast in my tent. Back on the bike I slogged on up the long hill not even looking out for any more VACANCIES signs. That was until I passed a superbly well lit up and altogether superb looking Guest House on my left hand side. Its sign read STUDIO ONE. Odd name for a Guest House I thought and continued pedalling. When I had gone a little way past it I felt somehow that I should go back and enquire about accommodation. Perhaps as an artist of over thirty years' standing it was the name of the place that was attracting me. It didn't occur to me for a moment that it could also indicate a connection with the many other forms of studio.

I went back, put the bike on its stand by the door and rang the bell. A man came to the door, listened to my request then said, "Wait here. I'll get my wife. She's boss of that side of things". I could almost hear the words of rejection in my head and was prepared to accept it without protest. Almost immediately a lady appeared and without question said, "Yes we can help you. Come in and have a look at the room." Overcome with gratitude I apologised for my appearance and insisted on taking off my Crocs before walking on the carpet. This was a Mrs Bree situation all over again! It was an immaculately furnished large room on the first floor with en suite bathroom. Of course I accepted it. She introduced herself as Sally. She explained that Stephen, her husband, was a lorry driver and had only just come in and was going to be off again at 4 am and that was how he couldn't really deal with my request. Back downstairs we joined Stephen who helped me take my luggage to my room and my bike into what appeared to be some sort of big store at the rear. "Your bike will be OK here" he assured me. "This place is all alarmed". By the time we had finished Sally had their supper on the table and insisted I join them.

Over supper I learnt that she was a professional artist who painted for national exhibitions and private commissions. All the bedrooms in the house were named after famous national artists. The room I was to occupy was named after the famous Basil Blackshaw whose portrait I had seen in the room but wasn't aware of its significance. When I mentioned the problems I had made for myself by carrying unnecessary clothing and equipment they both said that if there were any items I would like to leave with them until my return then I could do and reassured me that it would not be a problem.

In my bedroom I began another sort out of my things to see what else I might discard. First to go into the 'Leave Behind' pile were two pairs of lightweight trousers of the type with lots of pockets and zips at knee level to enable the bottom half of the legs to be removed. I had discovered that the zips severely rubbed my skin at knee level so much that the skin was red and quite sore. It was with some hesitation I decided to add my sleeping bag to the pile. It wasn't that it was too heavy; it was its bulk that I felt I could do without. I reasoned that as the nights were now getting shorter with the onset of summer they would also get warmer. Besides, if I needed any extra warmth I could wear some of my day clothes and if necessary put my waterproofs over them. I found lots of smaller items I could also discard. Finally I was satisfied that at last I had got it all about right. It was about 1 am when I got to bed. After breakfast Sally took me on a tour of Studio One to see the other rooms dedicated to the various famous artists then out the back to Sally's studio. That was where my bike had been kept overnight! Here I saw some of her beautiful paintings. I was so impressed with them that I felt a bit ashamed at having classed myself last night as an artist.

Just as I had got everything all set up to go a downpour of rain was in full swing. That was a good excuse for 'elevenses' with some of Sally's homemade cakes and my contribution of 'honey and yoghurt' bread I had bought the evening before. Using their bathroom scales I took the opportunity to calculate the combined weight of myself, the bike and the panniers now that I had shed all but the absolute necessities. It worked out at sixteen stone! Two hundred weight which I would be pedal pushing all the way around Ireland! I very much doubted that my legs would cope with all that pressure. Finally by midday the deluge had tapered off into a drizzle and I set off up the hill in a rather sad mood after such a happy and interesting overnight stay at Studio One. Despite my weight calculations earlier the bike felt much lighter today.

In no time at all I was in Groomsport, the sun was once more shining and there was no real wind to worry about. By the little harbour I bought an ice cream from a van that had just pulled in as I was taking a few photographs of the harbour and the super view out over the sea. Apart from myself and an elderly couple scoffing sandwiches and tea in their car there was no indication of it being the summer holiday season in that town.

South of Groomsport I saw an island not so far offshore and stopped to ask a man digging in a ditch at the side of the road about the island as it wasn't shown on my map. He said it was Copeland Island. When I asked if anyone lived there he said he didn't think so but people may well have lived there in the past. He went on to say that there were in fact three islands there even though I could only make out one. "It's a famous bird breeding place you know. There are even seals there at times and people come from all over the world to study bird life there. You can go out there if you get permission from the authorities but I think you can only stay a few hours. I've only been out there once myself and that was a long time ago" After a little pause he said, "That was when I was a boy". When I asked him he said his name was John.

I noticed that John was using a typical Irish long handled spade and shovel and asked him what he thought of the shorter handle versions of both which are used in England. "Sure those short things would ruin your back if you were using them all day. With these, you see, you can work away without being bent over. Besides, you have a longer reach with them if you are unloading sand or soil or anything small from the back of a cart". When I told him I had been using them all my adult life he said, "Well you know what I mean then don't you?" I told him about how, as children, we would use them as a sort of snow sledge in the winter down in Mourne. Some of the older lads could put one under each foot and do all sorts of fancy manoeuvres in the snow. He had never seen anyone doing that with the shovels he said. I told him about an occasion in England when I went into a hardware shop looking for such a shovel and the shopkeeper said to me, "You mean a gravediggers shovel don't you? I haven't seen one of them for years".

"Come on then" he said, "Show me how you can handle one". I was being put to the test. He stood holding my bike while I took the shovel and set about clearing a 4ft length of the ditch. I was doing this when a tourist bus came up the hill and slowed right down as it passed. I wasn't sure whether it slowed down because of the narrowness of the road or to let a passenger take a photograph of the pair of us. It must have been sight. Me, in all my fluorescent gear and helmet digging the ditch with this man standing watching holding my bike. I wonder which one of us looked like the workman and which one the tourist. Maybe we both looked like locals. Perhaps somewhere it will feature in someone's holiday snaps.

It was getting on for teatime as I arrived in Donaghadee. I rode out to the end of the long pier where there were about a dozen fishing boats and a few pleasure craft moored up on the high tide. I rode back along the pier to where there were a number of seats under a huge concrete roof. It was certainly a good practical shelter in inclement weather and an ideal spot for me to stop awhile and finish off my 'honey and yoghurt' bread from Bangor. Apart from two girls of about 11 or 12 years of age splashing about in a nearby paddling pool there was nobody about. A mangy and rather smelly dog came up to me and persisted in staying close by to see if I would share my snack with it. When I didn't he disappeared along the street obviously not very impressed. However, I was totally unprepared for the next development.

The two girls from the paddling pool appeared beside me. They eyed both me and the bike up and down. Before I had chance to say anything to them the first of a torrent of questions came forth as can often be the case with curious, innocent children. "Are you a tramp?" I managed to say, "No" but before I could elaborate there came: "Where do you sleep"? I replied, "In my tent"; "Why are you dressed like that? Where did you get that funny wee helmet"? I began to explain that I was cycling around the coastline of Ireland but got interrupted with, "Why are you doing that. Haven't you got a job"? I told them my age and that it was something I just wanted to do. "Oh, you're an explorer then are you?" The questions came thick and fast leaving no time for an answer. "Are you married? Do you have any kids? Why are you riding a bike? Don't you have a car? Are you famous? Did you ride your bike here from England? Are you English? Are you a Protestant? How many years will it take you to ride around Ireland? Are you going to sleep here tonight? Haven't you got any socks"? I did my best to answer most of their questions as we went along then suddenly the interrogation ended with, "Would you like us to sing you a song? We made it up last night" whereupon they went into a sort of little song and dance routine that lasted a few minutes. I had no idea what it was but I gave them a round of applause.

By this time I had expected the arrival on the scene of one or more concerned adults or parents but nobody did. This prompted me to intervene with a question to one of the girls. "Where are your parents?" Reply: "Oh I haven't got any. I'm an orphan". "Who do you live with?" I asked. "Me grandma" came the reply. I was getting into full swing now. "Where does your grandma live?" "Three doors down from the fish shop" came the reply. I gave up on that girl and said to the other. "And what about you. Where do you live?" "Four doors down from her". "And where are your parents?" "Me dad is in England and I don't know where my mother is". Well, I did my mighty best not to laugh at all this. However, I decided it was time for me to dispense a few kindly words of advice to this pair. "Hasn't anybody ever told either of you that you shouldn't go talking to strange men when you are on your own? It's not safe to do that". But back came the reply. "But you're not a strange man. You're an explorer aren't you?" I gave up. I got out my mobile 'phone. I told them that I couldn't talk to them any longer as I had to make a 'phone call and suggested they go back to the paddling pool whereupon they did there and then without a word. I couldn't help feeling just a little guilty at sending them away. A few minutes later as I rode off on my bike they came running to the footpath shouting, "Bye bye mister explorer". I don't think I will ever forget that encounter with those two cute innocent little Donaghadee girls.

On the road again I was now onto the Ards Peninsula heading for the village of Millisle. From a distance it looked like a huge caravan park with both mobile and static caravans on huge sites. Even though it was early evening I was sure that somewhere amongst this lot there would be a camp-site. I called into a small shop and enquired about camp-sites nearby. "I think there is one further up the road" the man said "but I think it is closed". I asked if he had any tent pegs. He hadn't but offered me some six inch screws which I bought just in case I didn't find any pegs further along the way. I had realised as I rode along earlier thinking about my first night's camping that the ground was quite hard. I had only got lightweight plastic tent pegs for both my tent and the tarpaulin. I now realised I needed long steel pegs especially for the tarpaulin which I intended putting over both the tent and my bike.

Soon I came to a road sign showing me that Ballywalter was 5 miles ahead; Ballyhalbert 9 miles and Portaferry 20 miles. I called at the site shop at Ballyferris Holiday Park. No, they didn't sell tent pegs. As I set off across the large car park towards the road I heard some girls voices calling, "Mister. Hey mister". I looked round only to discover that it was me they were calling. I cycled back to the two girls who were clearly out of breath with the running and the shouting. "Mister, you've left your bag at the shop". Well so I had. I had put my rucksack down by the shop door and hadn't picked it up when I came out. They ran off back into the shop before I could say anything to them. I found the girls in the shop and took them to the lady behind the counter where I thanked them and gave them 50p each to spend on whatever they fancied. They both thanked me. I left them deliberating over which sweets they fancied.

My next stop was a mile or so further on where I saw a man, accompanied by two young boys, busily working in the yard of a house near to the roadside. The house name I noted as Rosebank House. The man, called Will Hopes, who said he had just bought the place offered to let me camp in the garden overnight if I wished but he too wasn't aware of any camp-sites locally. I would have taken him up on his offer but I felt it was a bit too early

to set up camp. During our brief conversation I
mentioned my search for somewhere to buy some tent
pegs whereupon he said he would make me some from
some lengths of this steel he had in the barn. I declined
as I knew it would be hindering him in his work and
went back to the entrance. Just as I got there the two
boys came running after me with two metal tent pegs.
One said, "Daddy said these were in the barn and you
are to have them". I got out my purse to give them
something for them but they were already back with
their father. He saw what I was going to do and just
waved me away saying, "I hope you get some more
somewhere".

Another few miles along the road I came to Rockmore
Caravan Park but it didn't have a shop. On my way in I
passed a group of holiday makers setting up camp. They
were erecting a large awning between two caravans.
One of them spoke to me asking if I was looking for
anyone. I told him that I was looking for a shop which
sold tent pegs. He said there weren't any camp-sites this
side of Portaferry but as for tent pegs I could have as
many as I wanted when they had finished putting up
their awning. I joined in helping them and was treated to
a great mug of tea. They were all interested in the
journey I had undertaken and spoke in detail of the
various places I would visit around the coast. They said
they were from Newtonards and every summer went off
in their caravans.

As our conversation lengthened it transpired that they

knew my two brothers from their common involvement in tug-of-war competitions throughout Northern Ireland. They tactfully avoided my effort to establish any of their names but made a bit of a joke about it saying, "Your brothers will know us. You ask them when you see them". Next came an invitation to join them for a meal. It was one of my favourites, namely Shepherds Pie, but I declined their kind offer saying that I must move on and find a camping place before dark. At that stage one of the men selected a huge handful of straightest metal tent pegs and said I must take them. I selected 12 and put the rest back on the pile. Now came the awkward part when I tried to pay for them. It was refusals all the way around, even by the children but then I spotted a children's money box by the door of one of the caravans and put a few one pound coins in it before anyone could stop me. Then I was off on my bike to a round of best wishes from everyone.

The sun was getting close to setting by now. In the next village, called Ballywalter, I stopped at a small shop where I bought a few 'tasty bits' to have in my tent tonight. Shortly afterwards I came to Ballyhalbert. There was quite a bit of open coastline along the road. I decided that I wouldn't bother looking for a camp-site but instead would set up my tent in the first likely looking spot I came to before it got too dark. As I reached the top of a hill I saw a young man doing something with the front of a car in a driveway. As there were open fields along that stretch of road plus some rough land I stopped and told him of my intention of camping out somewhere along that stretch of road and asked if could advise me as to any particular place where I might be OK to do so. The fields by the side of the house looked ideal to me and I said so. He said the fields belonged to someone else but his parents would be able to help. At that he dashed indoors and came out with his elderly parents who insisted that I come inside. I couldn't really refuse.

They introduced themselves as Molly and Gordon Burn. Their son was Jonathan. I first had to explain briefly what I was doing whereupon they said I need look no further for a place to camp. I could set up my tent in their garden. They said it would be no problem to them. Over the mug of tea and plate of biscuits that appeared as if by magic I thanked them but said I wouldn't dream of setting up my tent in their immaculate garden. It included a large pond around which several prettily decorated tortoises were placed amongst an array of flowers. The decorated tortoises led Molly to tell me that Jonathan was an artist and of course I said I too was one and suggested he bring out a few of his painting to show me. This he did. They were beautiful original abstracts. With his permission I photographed some of them. Next he introduced me to his other hobby, namely the keeping of snakes. He produced from a cage at the back of the room a big dark coloured snake which was at least three feet long and four inches in diameter. He asked if I liked snakes and I said, rather evasively, that I didn't know anything about them really but wasn't too keen on them. At that he said, "Well this one is harmless. I'll show you". Before I could put down the mug of tea I had in one hand or the piece of cake in the other he had placed the snake around my shoulders. It felt quite heavy. I resisted a sudden urge to go to the bathroom as the snake's head came up level with my face and seemed to stare into my eyes. Jonathan suggested I should stroke it gently. I did and it made little shivery motions and proceeded to curl itself around my neck. I started to get worried when it began trying to get down into the collar of my waterproof jacket. Jonathan removed the big snake from me and replaced it with a slightly smaller one which moved rather quickly again around my neck area but I took courage and held it in both hands for a few minutes. Both snakes were eventually put back in their cage.

I could see that it was now dark outside and said that I would have to make a move but Gordon was already on the 'phone to somebody explaining about a man who was looking for somewhere to camp for the night. Molly said, "Gordon is speaking to friend of ours. He has a place down the road you can use". However, everything didn't seem to be going to well with the 'phone conversation. The friend seemed to be asking a lot of questions to which Gordon was doing his best to answer. "Yes he has a bike .... it's a big one .... No he is on his own........ No he's not young; he says he is seventy .... yes he's wearing all the proper gear including a helmet". Gordon put his hand over the 'phone and asked me, "What make is your bike?" I said it was a Giant. Gordon relayed this to the man. I sensed that there was a problem of some sort and was making frantic hand signs for Gordon to drop the matter but he persisted. "Yes its got four panniers and all that stuff".

There was something else being said to Gordon when he suddenly burst out laughing. "No he's not a Hells Angel biker. It's a pedal bike he's got. He originates from down in Mourne but lives in England". Everyone joined in at the laughing. That was it; no problem at all in using this other man's place.

Apparently a few years previously the man had let a few motor cyclists use this particular place of his down the road for one night. They turned out to be the Hells Angels variety and stayed almost a week during which time they caused him a load of bother. He thought I was another one of that ilk hence all the questions. Well, this was getting to be fun. In one day I was taken to be a tramp, an explorer and now a Hells Angel! Gordon and Molly were apologetic about the mistake but I reassured them by telling them the tale of the two little girls in Donaghadee who took me to be a tramp. We all had a good laugh at that.

They told me where to go to find this place by the roadside about a mile and a half further on. Jonathan said that he would give me time to get near it then he would join me on his motor bike to make sure I found the correct place. Handshakes all round and I was on my way to my first night in a tent. As good as his word Jonathan joined me just after the village street lights ended. He said he would go ahead and wait for me at the place. In about five minutes I joined him on a stretch of road where there were no street lights. He was sitting on his motor bike talking to a man at a gateway to a big house on the right hand side of the road. I drew up to them and John introduced us. The man's name was Robert. Almost on the opposite side of the road was on old house with its door and windows boarded up. Both said that there was flat ground at the back where I could put up my tent. It was now close to midnight but a full moon, still low on the horizon out over the sea provided plenty of light. I declined Robert's offer of supper but let him fill my plastic container with fresh water. Robert went indoors and Jonathan set off back home on his bike and I set about gaining access over the barbed wire which had been put up all along the front wall and gateway of the house. I explored the area on both sides of the house but there was barbed wire everywhere. Finally, after a struggle, I made it over the front garden wall and the barbed wire fence, complete with bike and panniers. There was a level piece of ground at the rear of the house. It opened directly onto the beach where the tide was gently lapping amongst the stones about twenty five yards away.

It took me about an hour to get the tent up, the bike laid out flat in front of it and the tarpaulin over both. Sure enough the plastic tent pegs I had brought from home would have been no use whatsoever on this hard ground. It took the metal pegs plus a fairly large stone which I used as a hammer to make it all secure. My final act was to take my four panniers from where I had left them by the house wall and placed them in the tent. With towel and flannel I went down to the beach and had a wash. It was so wonderful a moment there in the moonlight. Back at the tent I soon got snuggled down on my special mattress and felt warm enough in the few extra items of clothing I had put on. In a way I somehow felt more at ease than if I was in a sleeping bag. After the sandwiches I had at Mr and Mrs Burn's house I didn't feel hungry so saved my goodies for breakfast time.

When I reached out to switch off the small portable radio I put my hand on something very sticky instead of on the radio. I sat bolt upright switched on my torch to discover that there was a slug, about three inches long and an inch or more thick on my radio. I saw another one half way up the side of the tent just above my head. That was it. I began a search to see how on earth they could have got into the tent. Were they in the tent all the time? I checked the door zips but they were secure. I conducted the most thorough search of every square inch of the tent and altogether found five such slugs. I chucked them out and set about wiping up the slime they left behind and in doing so solved the problem of how they had got into the tent. Each of their slime trails began on one or other of the panniers. They had obviously crawled onto the panniers whilst they were on the grass by the house wall. I hadn't noticed them when I brought the panniers into the tent. Another lesson learnt and another vow made to never again make the mistake of not checking for slugs in similar situations. I was so thankful that I hadn't bothered to eat any supper. Even the thought of the consequences of finding a slug on one of my sandwiches was enough to make me sick. It didn't help matters when I shone my torch from the inside onto the sides and top of the tent to discover that at least ten or more big slugs were making their way up the outside of the tent. I think it was somewhere about 2.30am when I finally managed to get off to sleep, helped by the slow swishing sound of the waves on the beach but I felt sure I was going to have serious nightmares about snakes and slugs before the night was over. In the morning I removed the slug trails from the tent, and tarpaulin and packed up.

After a light breakfast I took a stroll along the beach in both directions. There wasn't much sand, just rocks and seaweed which somehow made it more interesting. Every type of plastic debris was there and had obviously been there for some time. There were about a dozen large wooden pallets strewn amongst the rocks as well, having no doubt been washed overboard from some ship. Everything was overgrown with seaweed. I kept an eye out for seals but didn't see any. It was a warm sunny morning and I wanted to linger on this stretch of beach for hours but felt it was time to be moving on southwards. I had another snack as it was nearing lunchtime. Robert came to see how I was doing and we chatted until about 2 pm. I was glad he came as I needed some help to get me and my outfit back over the barbed wire onto the road.

The sky clouded over as I was getting close to Portavogie. In Irish this name means 'Harbour of the bog' but I saw no evidence of bogs anywhere about this very smart looking little harbour town. It had quite a big harbour packed to capacity with brightly coloured fishing boats and just a few pleasure boats. I spoke to an elderly couple on a bench by the harbour. They said they had both lived there all their lives. I asked about the bogs. They said that there was little sign left of the so called bogs. Everywhere is being built on now they said. It is new houses everywhere but we don't want it to turn into another Bangor or Newcastle. "Do you know" the man said, "There were over eighty windmills along this Ards peninsula at one time but now there are only a few. You passed one in down in Millisle on your way here but it's only a show-piece now". I asked about the type of fish being caught. "It's mainly prawns and herrings but these cutbacks on how often boats can be fishing are a real problem". A quick shower of rain sent the couple to a nearby car and me back on the road out of the town towards today's target of Portaferry.

I couldn't help but admire the brightly painted house, even the farm buildings, as I rode along on this most pleasant stretch of road which had its fair share of sharp little hills and sharp turns but the traffic was light on this Saturday morning, the 2nd of May. The village was an artist's paradise with its beautiful coloured roadside cottages and the sea right there almost at the side of the road. I turned off to my left along a narrow road signed Manse Road but I feared it might be a one way route so I asked for directions from a woman leading a small calf on a rope along the road. When I mentioned Portaferry she said that as I was a stranger to the area I should stay back up on the main road. "It's a total maze down there" she said, "Take my advice and go on the main road". I asked where this road went to. "It goes nowhere" she said, "It wanders all round with lots of other roads joining in such as ......". Here she rattled off several place names and road names. I explained briefly what I was intending to do over the next few weeks or months. She wished me luck, gave me a handful of sweets from a paper bag and turned off down a lane way. Well, her advice was spot on. Over the next hour I must have turned down five or six small roads which all turned out to lead to farm houses. Somehow I passed the same golf course twice! I had visions of finishing up back in Cloghy when at last I spotted a sign pointing to Portaferry. It was on a road called Bar Head Road. In the far distance I could just make out street lights in the gathering dusk and felt sure I had struck gold. It had to be Portaferry.

I then met a man pushing a wheelbarrow with a collie dog in it. I stopped to check that the lights I could see were at Portaferry. He said that yes that was Portaferry. I commented about the dog riding in the wheelbarrow and asked if it was ill or injured. I said I was well used to seeing people walking dogs and even some people who carried small dogs in a bag but never one in a wheelbarrow. "Ah no" he said. "He's been doing that since he was a pup. Now he insists on jumping into it when I'm going down to the shed or anywhere. I think he's lazy you know. I've been thinking about getting a little donkey and cart then we both can have a ride". I said I thought that was an excellent idea and maybe one that I should have considered instead of the bike. He shook my hand wished me luck in Portaferry and strode off into the darkness.

Sure enough an aptly named Shore Road got me into Portaferry. But nowhere had I seen a camp-site but by now I was learning that in these rural areas there are no such places as camp-sites. They were all near to big seaside towns and inland where there were walking and hiking places. It wasn't until about ten minutes after I parted from the man that I realised I had missed a golden opportunity to get his advice on somewhere I could pitch my tent for the night. No doubt he had a farm of some sort where I could have set up camp.

I had originally intended to ride around the shore of Strangford Lough but the more I thought about it the more I realised that of course it wasn't a coastal route as such and if I was to cycle all similar routes on this trip then I wouldn't be back in the UK until Christmas! I had some great friends in Newtownards called Carole and Eddie who were expecting me to call but I decided I would tell them later of my decision. Now I had to decide on where I was going to stay that night. I went into the big combined shop and petrol station in the main square to buy a tourist type book that might show camping sites but they didn't have one. I asked a few of the customers about camp-sites but they couldn't help either. I went back outside to enjoy a big bar of chocolate I had just bought and to see if fate would help me decide what to do next. Sure enough it did, as in Bangor at Studio One.

The car parking area was full of vehicles but somehow my attention got focused on a large dark 4x4 parked almost in the centre of the car park. I could see a woman in the passenger seat. It was quite a busy time and people were coming and going in cars etc. as I looked around but my attention kept coming back to the woman in the 4x4. Leaving my bike where it was by the supermarket doorway I made my way across to the 4x4. As I got to it I saw a little child in the seat behind her. The vehicle was facing me and I knew she could see me but as I got up to her vehicle she ignored me until I knocked on the window. She lowered it slightly and I asked her if she knew of anywhere that I might be able to camp for the night and quickly explained what I was doing. She said that she wasn't aware of any camp-sites around Portaferry but just as she was telling me a younger woman appeared. She was obviously the driver. She said, "Mum, what's the matter?" as she looked at me in my bright cycling outfit and helmet. I could see she was very curious, to put it mildly, as to why I was at her vehicle. I saved her mother from answering the question by firstly introducing myself and what I was doing then briefly telling her daughter about looking for a camp-site. "Oh", she said, "You gave me a scare just then. I thought there was something wrong. I saw you going to our car and imagined you were a policeman or traffic warden of some sort". Then "Wait a minute while I put these things in the car".

Having done that she then said, "Well you need look no further for a campsite or anything like that. My name is Mary and this is my mum, also called Mary. We live a few miles out of town on the Strangford Lough shore and right now we have a great big barbecue in full swing at the farm. We have come up to the supermarket here for more stuff so you can come down right now and join us. It is by our big beach hut on the shore of the lough and tonight when we have finished you can make yourself at home in the hut. You can stay all weekend if you want. No arguing, you must come. My husband Peter and all of us would love to have you. Promise you'll come". I was totally flabbergasted at this turn of events. No way could I see me joining a big family barbecue in this outfit but she was so persuasive and didn't seem to be the type to take no for an answer. She refused to listen to my reasons for not taking her up on her ever so kind offer. I felt it would, in the circumstances, be unreasonable to refuse so I said I would. "Right" she said, "It won't take you long" then proceeded to give me explicit instructions on my tape recorder on how to get to their farm called Half Hill Dairy Farm in Abbacy Road, Portaferry. She even gave me their telephone number just in case I needed any help in finding them. Then they were gone.

I dashed back into the shop and used their toilets to get changed out of my riding gear and into the few items of 'ordinary' clothing I was carrying. Next I bought a few bottles of what I thought might be acceptable wine and set off following the instructions on my tape recorder. I was about half way there when Mary and another lady reappeared in their car. She apologised for not offering to take my panniers so that the ride to their place would be easier. "The other reason I came was that I thought you might not come after all. Everyone is waiting to meet you". Before they set off she said that I must be careful when I arrived as they had a Rottweiler guard dog which didn't take kindly to strangers. "But don't worry. We'll be there to meet you at the farm gate". Then off they went. I rode along with my mind in a whirl. I was just so amazed at my good fortune tonight. It seemed just such a coincidence but then in a way, such coincidences were not anything new in my life. But that is a another story for another time.

On arrival at the farm gate I saw the house door open and then hurtling towards me came the Rottweiler barking furiously, closely followed by Mary. Needless to say I stayed at the gate, in fact stood well back from it. A few shouts from Mary had the big dog standing there staring at me, giving a low steady growl all the time. From previous experience of dogs of all sorts I knew the value of talking to them in a quiet voice and that was what I did while Mary reached the gate and opened it. The Rottweiler, a bitch, was called Mia. I made peace with her by giving her a piece of the chocolate bar I had bought earlier. She calmed down then and eventually let me stroke her and from that moment she stayed by my side up to the farmhouse and whilst I deposited my bike in the barn then accompanied Mary and her mum down a lane way to the beach where the barbecue was definitely in full swing. First I was introduced to Peter and then to everyone in turn. In no time I had a drink in hand and told to join in and help myself to anything I liked. There were at least a dozen people there but there were enough of various meats and sausages on the barbecue plus a table laden down with more food in the beach hut, to feed the population of

Portaferry. . The beach hut was big enough to seat all of us and was fitted out like a modern kitchen. All evening Mia continued to stay by my side and I rewarded her with the occasional snippets from my plate and kept stroking her. I felt sure we were friends. Everyone wanted to know the why and wherefores of my intended trip around Ireland. They were clearly amused when I told them some of the funny incidents I had experienced so far. They were a wonderful group of people who made me feel so comfortable in their company.

If the meeting up with Mary and her mum were not enough of a coincidence there was more to come. At one stage the conversation in the group turned to holidays abroad. I mentioned visiting Chile. Almost with one voice a few in the group said "Chile. Why do you go there"? I explained that I went out there once a year to visit my son Peter and his family. The next question was, "Where in Chile does he live". I said that he at first lived in Santiago but he now lived in up in the north of the country in a town called La Serena. It transpired in the excited conversation which followed that a cousin of Peter (Mary's husband) had married a girl from La Serena and they now lived in Santiago. Most of the group had recently been to the wedding in La Serena. Further conversation revealed that the young lady lived only a few streets away from Peter and the family. Everyone was as amazed as I was at this coincidence. So often when I mention Chile I get responses which vary from "Where is Chile?" to "Don't you worry about being in Africa with all the trouble there". But to be at a barbecue on the shores of

Strangford Lough with a group of strangers and to suddenly find we had something like that in common. We were all amazed at the coincidence. To me the initial attraction which drew me to approach Mary's mother in their car earlier that evening in Portaferry now made sense. Over the years I have got used to this sort of thing happening.

It was close to 1am when everyone got set and ready to leave. Mary and Peter, unknown to me, had gone up to their house and brought back a sleeping bag, pillows and blankets for me to use. I was left surrounded by loads of food of all description and told help myself. They even left the fire smouldering outside so that I could sit at it if I wished. Peter's parting words were, "You are coming up for breakfast. I'll come down for you". Mia didn't go with them. As they left they called to her but she just stood looking after them and then back to me as much as to say, "Why are you leaving him?" I went and sat by the fire for about an hour while Mia lay beside me looking totally content. It was a calm warm night with the moon, now high in the sky, reflected in the smooth waters of the lough. Occasionally I heard a bird calling somewhere in the distance. I could not have felt more at ease and at home as I did there in that beautiful location with such great memories of the day on which to reflect.

Eventually I went into the hut and laid out the sleeping bag on the floor. Mia followed me and lay down by the door. I offered her some bits from the plates of food thinking that was why she had stayed with me but she refused my offerings. I closed the door, laid out my sleeping bag and laid down. By that time Mia was already laid stretched out and fast asleep. What a dog! During the night I woke up to find Mia's face very close to mine which startled me at first. She was just staring at me. I spoke to her and sat up. Had I been snoring I wondered? Did she think there was something wrong with me? She didn't show any signs of wanting to go out into the night but I nevertheless opened the door and encouraged her to go out. She did with what I sensed was reluctance. I watched as she again stood looking up the lane way towards the farmhouse then back to where I was at the door. After a few minutes of this she went off up towards the farmhouse. I took it she had gone home. She probably had had enough of my snoring. I closed and fastened the door and was soon back asleep.

I was awakened by a group of screeching seagulls on the roof of the beach hut about 9 am. I stepped outside to sample the fresh morning air and admire the absolutely beautiful and tranquil view across the Lough. But the first thing I saw was my Rottweiler pal Mia lying fully stretched out in the morning sun by the embers of last nights fire. She was fast asleep. Very quietly I took a photograph of her. I guessed she had been up home and had come back to check on me only to find that she was locked out. I brought her out some titbits and as I put them beside her she woke up but wasn't really interested in my offerings. Together we went for a walk along the beach in the fresh morning air. Away to the south a morning mist was lifting off the Mourne Mountains. As

I stood there looking at them I felt excited at the prospect of being back up there in Mourne within the next few days.

I was tidying up in the beach hut when Peter and Mary arrived in their car to take me for breakfast. I told them about Mia. Apparently she hadn't been up to the house at all. Her supper hadn't been touched. Now I felt really sorry for her. She must have come back to join me only to find that she was locked out! Poor Mia! Up at the farmhouse I watched as the dog tucked into her meal.

Over a tasty breakfast Peter and Mary were setting out their plans for the day. Mary was going out later with the children but they both urged me to stay another night. "Why don't you treat yourself to a weekend break? Surely you must be ready for it. We won't be using the beach hut for at least another month so you can stay as long as you like?" I agreed to stay another night but said I didn't want to be bothering him as I felt sure he was a very busy man. He said he would like to show me around their dairy farm and see their show horses. "We'll do that tomorrow" he said. "We'll let you relax and do your own thing today". Well, how could I refuse such an offering, and yes I felt as I could do with a break from the cycling. It would get me all rested for going up to Mourne where I knew from experience it would be all late nights, partying and going out dancing.

Back at the beach hut I sat out in the sun and read

'Strangford Shores; Paintings and Stories From Around The Lough' by Alison Brown and Jane C. M. Crosby. I had another long walk along the beach then did some writing of postcards and a few letters. My final pleasure was watching the sunset out over the Lough. This was a day to dream about; like a mini holiday. I watched clouds settling over Slieve Donard. That was a sure sign that it would be raining tomorrow. Mia came down to check on me three times that afternoon then finally as I was getting ready for an early night but she didn't stay. She probably had had enough of my snoring!

Sure enough it was raining when I first woke up so I went back to sleep. I had only woke up for the second time when Peter came. He took me up to the farmhouse to join the family for breakfast. Afterwards he showed me the dairy and explained how the cows got lined up in their stalls with the help on an ingenious system of swinging bars, all operated systematically as each cow took her place in long row to await the milking machines being attached to their udders. He showed me the computer system which did all sorts of calculations and analysis of the milk coming from each individual cow before it was collected in various large tanks ready for sale. A type of floor level conveyor belt, positioned all the way along behind the cows, made the clearing out of their manure a very simple, efficient and hygienic operation. No need for shovels forks and brushes here! What a far cry from what I had seen on our farm when the milking was done by hand by either my father or my mother sitting on a low stool getting the milk into a bucket and at the same time humming a tune or singing.

Apparently the singing made the cows relax which helped the process. The cleaning out of the stalls was very much a manual labour job with shovel, brush and wheelbarrow. I told Peter about my parents singing to the cows and jokingly asked him if he ever did that. He said, "You would have to be a Mario Lanza and have a good loudspeaker system to be heard over the noise they make in here at milking time".

Next came 'elevenses' at the farmhouse then it was down to the stables with Peter to see the horses. He gave feed to several fine looking horses in their stalls then took me to see the stallion called 'Come T'. It was an absolute beauty of a horse, white all over and in immaculate condition. I had never been so close to such a fine big horse which, in its surroundings, looked huge. It towered over us both in the confines of the stall but I must say that I didn't venture any closer than the stall door. It never took its eyes off me and I'll admit I was more than just a little nervous being so near to it. When Peter said he was going to take 'Come T' out of his stall and put him in a nearby field I made a quick exit from the stable into the yard where I positioned myself near a low gate that I felt I could climb over quite quickly if the need arose. However, Peter brought him out on a halter about 6ft long. I felt much safer on seeing Peter using a halter especially as they were both going to pass within about 10 ft. of where I was standing.

Suddenly, as they were level with me, 'Come T' reared up on its hind legs, at the same time making a terrible screeching sound. Its mouth was wide open and his big eyes staring. It literally walked on its back legs all the time pawing the air wildly with its front legs. I felt for the top bar of the gate in preparation for when it was going to break loose from Peter and charge at me. I need not have worried. Peter let this go on for about a whole minute then said quietly, "That's enough now Come T. Stop it". The horse immediately dropped back on all fours and stood still. I could feel my heart beating with the scare I got. I wished I had had my camera with me to photograph the horse's performance but then I would have been too scared to even think of using it. When Peter re-joined me from the nearby field I apologised for obviously disturbing the horse when it saw me in the yard. "You didn't scare him. That was all a big performance because he knew you were a stranger. It's his party piece when we have him at shows. He wouldn't harm you". Peter could obviously see that I had had a scare. As we headed back to the farmhouse Peter told me of the many prizes 'Come T' had won at shows all over Ireland and the UK. I wasn't surprised one bit. Over a mug of tea and home-made cake at the house I was treated to a display of all sorts of medals and prize memorabilia connected with 'Come T' and the other horses. This included traps and harness of all sorts and sizes and colours. It was now mid-afternoon and it had started to rain steadily, a sure sign that it was going to be raining all evening. Both Peter and Mary persuaded me that I should have another night in the beach hut then make an early start the following morning. I knew they were spoiling me but I was enjoying it. What a kind couple they were. I enjoyed their company so much. I adjourned to the beach hut once more and had a siesta;

my first since I had started this trip.

About an hour later I was woken up by Peter accompanied by Mia. The rain had stopped. "Come on" he said, "We have another treat for you". He was as good as his word. We went down to the field to put the stallion back into its stable for the night. I waited where I had been before and saw Peter catch him in the field and lead it back up to its stable. I stood where I had been before and sure enough, when they drew level with me the 'Come T' did a repeat performance but this time he added a front leg stands and thrashed out wildly with both back legs, all the time making that loud screeching sound. Again a few words from Peter ended the show. "Would you like to lead him to his box?" said Peter. Obviously I declined. I felt sure there was a hint of a smile on both their faces. When I felt it was safe to do so I followed them to Come T's box. "Watch" said Peter. "I have put him in some new straw bedding. See what he does". 'Come T' sniffed it then promptly lay down and rolled over and over a few times before getting back up. "You see, he's very fussy about his bedding". It was then back to the house and a delicious Sunday dinner with all the family. Mary and Peter were the perfect hosts. The chat and talk went on until very late. Peter wouldn't hear about me walking down to the beach hut in the dark and so it was more star treatment by taking me down in the car. What a day that had been!

Next morning I was all packed and ready when I discovered that my credit card was missing. It was now panic stations! I knew I last used it in Portaferry but that was all. I checked all my pockets and didn't find it so it was everything back out of the panniers again but still no trace. I even searched the whole of the floor and the ground outside. My panic forced me to make another check of all my pockets. To my immense relief I found it in one of the large pockets in my waterproof coat. How I had missed finding it the first time I don't know. By the time I had got everything back together I had hoped to have been well on my way. Up at the farmhouse the whole family turned out to see me off. They couldn't have made me feel more welcome if I had been one of their own. But where was my guardian Mia? As Mary came to open the farmyard gate the dog came running at top speed to my side. I gave her the last piece of the chocolate which I had bought in Portaferry. I had saved it all weekend for her. She gently took it from my hand. I shook her front paw to say a special farewell to my very special lovely canine friend. Away down at the end of the laneway I looked back and there she was still at the farm gate with Mary. I rode off with a lump in my throat. What a wonderful few days I had spent there at Half Hill Dairy Farm. Surely those few days there would be the highlight of my trip?

Back in Portaferry I boarded the ferry boat and within twenty minutes was in Strangford. The fare was one pound ten pence. I expected it to be at least a few pounds. I was having a problem with my IPhone which I couldn't resolve but there wasn't a shop in Strangford which could sort it for me. I was advised to go to Downpatrick where I was assured there was an O2 shop which could deal with it. There was nothing else I could do but go on to Downpatrick, get the problem resolved then come back to Strangford and resume my coastal route. It was a sixteen mile round trip but I didn't care. In case of an emergency it was important to have both my mobile phones working perfectly. Back in Strangford I resumed my journey from where, a few hours ago, I had landed from the ferry. I set off along Stella Maris Street which I took to be the start of the road along the coast but it just brought me back again further on to the Shore Road which I had been on in the first place.

Familiar place names from the days when I worked in the Mourne Observer Newspaper in Newcastle were now on the signposts ahead. Soon the Shore Road became the Ardglass Road which took me along the actual coastline. For the first time I began to feel an ache in my wrists which I could only attribute to too much weight on them so I lowered the seat and raised the handlebars to see if that would help. The afternoon was quickly slipping into evening as the Shore Road led me past Killard Point then into Ballyhornan. A short way past Ballyhornan I saw a fairly large island a short distance from the shore. My map identified it as Guns Island. Apparently it got its name in the early 1700s when 'Ametie', a French ship carrying guns to support the rebellion in those years, ran aground on the nearby rocks with only one survivor.

I got into Ardglass about 4 pm and rode around by the

marina. Everywhere looked so neat and tidy and painted in bright colours. There were not many people about and all the shops seemed to either be shut or about to do so. I decided not to stop but to push on towards Killough on the main road. I had hoped to make it to Newcastle where I would stay with my sister-in-law Betty overnight but I knew that it was going to be too late to be calling on her. I would leave that until the next day and stop somewhere near Dundrum instead. I didn't feel like stopping to make something to eat so I kept a look out for a shop where I could get in something for tea and supper. Outside Killough I saw a woman doing something at the front gate of a bungalow. I stopped and asked her if there was a cafe or anywhere similar further along the road where I could get a sandwich and perhaps a cup of tea. She looked me up and down, didn't answer my question but instead said, "Are you a tourist of some sort. You have a lot of bags on that bike?" I very briefly told her what I was doing. "And where are you sleeping at night?" I said that so far I had slept in my tent which wasn't strictly true but I didn't want to go into details. "Oh you poor man. Forget about looking for a cafe around here" she said. "There isn't one. I have just made something to eat for me and my husband. Come in and have something with us and tell us all about your adventure". I tried to decline her offer saying that I wanted to move on towards Dundrum before it got dark but I could see she wasn't going to take no for an answer as she made off towards her door saying, "Come on. We won't keep you long. It's all on the table". So I followed her. Her husband was already sitting at the kitchen table which was indeed set out with sandwiches and cake plus some delicious looking home-made iced buns. She had me to sit at the table and almost immediately cutlery, plates, cup and saucer, even a napkin, were in front of me. The tea was poured and two big sandwiches and two iced buns were on the plate. "Now get stuck into that". I did as I was told.

Her husband just smiled but never spoke a word except to say "Hello". To me he looked ill. His wife sat between us and plied me with questions. When I told her I was originally from Mourne she spoke of people in Kilkeel whom she knew and of relatives in Annalong but although she mentioned their surnames I didn't know any of them. I finished off the two sandwiches as quickly as I could but tried not to make it look as if I was in a hurry. As soon as I had eaten one of the two buns she put another one in its place but I said I was full and couldn't eat anything else, including another bun even though they were one of my favourite pastries. Another cup of tea followed then I said that I must push on. I got out my tape recorder and asked if I could have their names as I was thinking of writing a book about my travels and would like to mention their kindness. "You can put that thing away. You are not having our names. Before we know it you might have our names on the radio or on the television or even in the 'papers". I did as she commanded. She wouldn't even disclose their first names but she did it in a nice way so as not to offend me. I got my helmet back on and as I got to the door I discreetly put a few pound coins behind a vase on the hall table. She followed me out to the gate. As I said my thanks and got all set to ride off she handed me one of those old fashioned looking brown paper bags.

"You've got a few buns in there" she said, "Plus that money you tried to hide on the hall table. Keep it and put it towards a pair of socks. I can't believe you are riding in the rain and cold without anything on your feet". Before I could make any comment she took my arm and planted a big wet kiss on my cheek. "May the good Lord look after you son. Now get off" and was away up the path to her front door. All I could do was shout a word of thanks after her. I saw her look around and took the opportunity to blow her a kiss. She waved and went in the door. What a woman!

The run into Killough was not as hilly as I expected it would be but the problem was a steady drizzle of rain that looked as if it might go on all evening. I had to stop and investigate a rattling sound at the back end of the back which turned out to be the bike stand. The bolts holding it in place had worked loose somehow but also the legs were slightly buckled. It must have been caused by all that weight it was holding up at the beginning of my trip. I tried to tighten the bolts but the threads were also wrecked. I removed it and later dumped it in a roadside bin in Dundrum.

North of Dundrum I called at Byrnes Market Garden Centre where I met the proprietor Gerrard Byrne. I had seen a field on the hill beside his place as I passed by and thought it would be an ideal place to set up camp for the night. However, it wasn't his field but straightaway he said I could camp overnight on the lawn in the Centre. The lawn was by the side of his house. He said I could have full use of all the usual customer facilities such as the toilets and the drinks machine. The staff were closing the Centre for the night as Gerrard and I chatted about all sorts but in particular our shared interest in travelling abroad. He took my mobiles to get them charged up overnight but returned to invite me in for tea. I declined saying that I had some food I should eat and that I really needed an early night. Nevertheless as I was setting up my tent they brought me out a mug of tea and a plate stacked with some very tasty looking sandwiches. I had only got all set up when the rain came. I didn't care as I was snug, warm and content with the tea, sandwiches plus the bag of buns the lady at Ardglass gave me. I scoffed the lot before settling down for the night. As the Garden Centre was opening the next morning I thanked Mr and Mrs Byrne, had some photographs taken together and in no time was back on the road to Newcastle with Dundrum Bay glittering in the morning sunshine. At Clough I took a photograph of the sign: 'You Are Entering Mourne' which according to maps is technically correct but I think almost everyone regards the start of Mourne as being where the Slieve Donard meets the road after leaving Newcastle when going towards Kilkeel. In fact there is another sign near there which states: 'Welcome To Mourne'.

Up head Slieve Donard, the highest in the Mourne range at 852 metres, loomed above Newcastle. On the way into the town I stopped briefly at my first workplace, the offices of 'The Mourne Observer', then off again along the newly designed and modernised promenade which I was viewing for the first time. The tide was out and the beach was crowded which was normal for that time of year. With sadness I saw that the Palace Cinema, where I worked every evening after my day job with the newspaper, has now been replaced by a row of shops. The Brownville Hotel next door to the Palace Cinema, which was my 'digs' for those three years, had now been converted into a house. I treated myself to an ice cream and sat on the Shimna River Bridge watching the holiday makers going past. Then it was to my sister-in-law's house for tea followed by a few hours of me and Betty going back over the years when Johnny, my late brother, was alive and we lived near each other in North London. At Betty's I had my second night in a proper bed since 'Studio One' at Bangor.

Next morning, after bidding Betty good bye, it was into town for a haircut. I didn't think I really needed one but perhaps it would help improve my appearance amongst friends and family up in Mourne later that day. Of course I just had to go into Newcastle's one and only 'Cycle Shop' where I had a browse amongst the latest cycles on the market and bought a replacement cycle chain, another cycle stand and some lubricating oil. My final trip down memory lane was to see Martin Waddell and his wife Rosaleen. Martin and I were apprentices together in the Mourne Observer. He went on to become a famous author with both national and international awards to his name and plays on television and screen. After a very pleasant few hours together I was off up past The Rock and on my way into Mourne proper. The road along this stretch towards Glasdrumman runs high above the beach with super views out to sea and of course up the mountain sides on the right. The latter gives way to fields and pretty houses and cottages the closer you get to Glasdrumman. Out at sea there were a few little of boats obviously involved in attending to lobster pots. About half way to Glasdrumman I crossed the famously named Bloody Bridge then into Annalong which is one of the busiest and most well-known fishing towns of its size along the east coast of Ireland. I stopped at 'Nisas' supermarket and got stocked up on my fast dwindling supply of sweets and chocolates then had a welcome cup of tea and a few tasty pancakes in the aptly named 'Top Nosh' cafe before moving along towards Kilkeel. This short journey from Newcastle towards Kilkeel evoked so many memories for me of my cycling to home and back at weekends over the three years I worked in Newcastle but in those days I would have done it in half the time it was now taking me. Twenty one geared bike hadn't been invented in those days. My all-time favourite then was one fixed gear which meant non-stop pedalling.

It was unusually cold that morning in comparison with previous days on the way here. In Glassdrumman a cold shower of rain started so I took shelter in a shop. Within minutes the rain turned into a really heavy shower of hailstones. I couldn't believe it could change so quickly. A few local men and women shoppers waited with me in the doorway until the shower cleared during which time we covered quite a few topics from the weather and of course what I was doing. Their consensus of opinion on my journey was that I was mad to be doing what was alright for youngsters but not for a man of seventy! The hailstone shower eventually cleared and out came the sun to welcome me into my home town of Kilkeel. I had a quick ride down to the harbour to have a look at the fishing boats but there were only two there and they were being repaired by a very busy group of men. I asked a woman, who was taking photographs of the harbour, where were all the fishing boats. "All out somewhere in the North Sea I suppose" she said casually. "I believe they are back at the weekend". Her accent wasn't local so I assumed she was a visitor so I asked where she was from. "Oh I live near here. I'm an artist. I've come down especially to get a picture of the harbour without the boats". At that I mentioned my own involvement with art and so a conversation ensued but was interrupted after about five minutes by the arrival a man in a car and she was gone with him before I could get her name. We hadn't got around to introducing ourselves but I do think somehow she mentioned that her name was Cathy and that she specialised in painting scenes of the Mournes with the local art club. This was where I broke away from my coastal route and headed up the Moyadd Road into the heart of Mourne to have a few days with my two brothers Francis and Martin. My sister Kathleen lives in Rostrevor but I was sure I would meet up with her before then in one or both of my two brother's homes.

The following Monday I resumed my travels. My first stop was my parents' grave at Massforth Cemetery in Kilkeel. From there I went back to the town centre and off towards Greencastle situated near the well-known wartime airfield called Cranfield. It was fairly busy

down by the pier. I enquired from a small group of
people there if boats still crossed over to Greenore,
Omeath and Carlingford on the southern shore of
Carlingford Lough as they did in my childhood days.
"Oh yes they do, but it's mainly to Greenore. It's not so
much in the winter as in the summer. If you wait a while
that boat coming in will be taking us across. You can
come with us. They'll take your bike. They take motor
bikes and cars too you know". I said I was off to
Rostrevor now and briefly told them of my coastline
trip. One said, "You should take a shortcut across here
and save yourself going all that way up round Newry
and all that lot". It was tempting but I had arranged to
stay one night with my sister in Rostrevor and wouldn't
miss that opportunity that for any reason.

I had to backtrack to Cranfield then head westwards
along the Benagh Road which took me back up the very
busy Newry Road. Next was Killowen. I was cycling
along there quite steadily when I was joined by a young
man, dressed in a really professional cycling outfit
riding a racing track type bike with no panniers and
carrying nothing but a very small bag on his back. He
was a 19 year-old called Eddie from Castlewellan doing
a circular tour of the perimeter of the Mourne
Mountains. He was in a cycling club but today's run was
just to help keep him fit for the more serious track
events. He rode with me for about a half mile while we
chatted. I shared one of my chocolate bars with him as
we rode along. He did most of the talking as I was
getting out of breath trying to keep pace with him but I
was conscious he was just being polite to a fellow

cycling enthusiast. I urged him to push on as I wasn't bothered about time like he was so off he went, bent low over his handlebars, his legs going round like propellers. I felt that if I was able to cycle at that speed all day I would be able to go around Ireland in one week or maybe less!

In most places the view across Carlingford Lough from the Newry Road into Rostrevor is obstructed by trees but nevertheless those glimpses I got showed the Lough's waters gleaming a dark blue in this afternoon sunshine. I only saw one boat, which was laden with large containers, heading inland towards the large ports of either Warrenpoint or Newry. I had cycled this road from my earliest childhood days when I would ride into Warrenpoint to have a treat at the Genoa Cafe where my sister Kathleen had been a waitress for years before she got married and came to work in the Roxburgh Hotel in Rostrevor. Most time I cycled there from Atticall 'through the mountains' as it was known, meaning via Spelga and Hilltown then went home via the Kilkeel Road. Often Kathleen's husband Dan McAlinden, who was a Rostrevor taxi owner/driver, would 'run me out home' if it got too late to be cycling the thirteen mile trip in the dark.

At Kathleen's it was food and talking until bedtime. The following morning early, after a very tasty and wholesome breakfast I was off. She came to the top of her street to wave me off as I went towards the Ross Memorial and Warrenpoint. I felt more than a twinge of sadness at leaving not only Mourne but especially my beloved sister Kathleen. From here on into my trip I had no family to look forward to seeing. However, in Cork I would hopefully be meeting up with a friend, John Lawlor and his family, whom I had known many years ago in England.

Warrenpoint is a quite busy town with a good mixture of holiday makers to and from the Mourne area plus those who avail themselves of the popular fifteen minute ferry service across the Lough to Omeath plus guided tours up and down the Lough. I paused for a few minutes, for old times' sake, in The Square. The Genoa Cafe, where my Kathleen worked, was still there and as busy as ever. Next stop along the route was Newry which is reputedly the fourth largest city in Northern Ireland and the eighth largest in the whole of Ireland. The River Clanrye runs through it and into Carlingford Lough. I avoided going into its busy city centre and simply kept turning left until I was over the Clanrye River Bridge. From there I kept to the road nearest to the river, until I came into Omeath. The road was rough and once again my wrists began to ache from the constant vibration but there was little I felt I could do to lessen the problem. From Omeath down to Carlingford and Greenore I had clear view of the Mourne Mountains all the way across the Lough. From Greenore, using my binoculars, I could actually see my childhood homeplace in Atticall. I can remember when, on a clear day, without binoculars we could see Greenore from our farmhouse. Of course it was easy to see across to Greencastle and its harbour where I was the day before.

Just short of Greenore I saw a fair sized hill on my right with a lane running up the side of it from where, I reckoned, I could get a much better view of Mourne with my binoculars. I left my bike a little way up the lane from the road and walked up to the top of the hill. Sure enough my binoculars gave me a clear view of the Atticall area including the spire of the new Atticall Church. I didn't feel in any hurry to move on and had a drink of my sister's tea from a small flask I had acquired earlier in Rostrevor. I was enjoying this when I heard a man calling to his dog on the lane way almost beside me. I was a bit bothered as I was trespassing in someone's field and thought it might be the owner. I walked back to the field gate. It wasn't the owner of the field but another local man herding about a dozen sheep down towards the main road. I joined him and told him what I was doing. He had his collie dog to stop the sheep going any further and asked if he could have a look through my binoculars. I showed him how to adjust them to his eyesight. He walked with me back to my earlier viewpoint and stood surveying the countryside below and away across in the Mourne Mountains. He was really impressed with my binoculars and asked me lots of questions about them. He was in no hurry and was enjoying the chat. So was I. He said his name was Martin but he was known locally by a nickname but didn't seem to want to tell me what it was and I didn't press him on the subject. He talked about when he was a 'young fellow' he often went over to 'The Point' (Warrenpoint) with other lads. "They had great rides then in 'The Point'. I couldn't even look at them now I'd be that dizzy" he said. He told me about his first girlfriend being from Warrenpoint. "It was alright in the summer months" he said, "when the boats were running but when the winter came the boats didn't run that often and I couldn't get to see her. A few times I missed the last boat and got into real trouble at home over it all so I had to give her up". I asked why he couldn't have cycled around via Newry to see her. "You must be joking" he said, "No girl would be worth biking all that way to see. Besides, I didn't have a bike". As we walked back to his sheep he asked me more about the binoculars. He said that now that he had had a good look through them he fancied getting a small pair like mine. "You see" he said, "My eyesight is no good now and I have to get up close even to count the sheep. Another problem is that in the summer and at lambing time there are always all sorts of townie people up around here with dogs. They don't have them under control. Now if I had a pair of those binoculars I could keep an eye on such folk without having to be too near to them. That's done it, I'm in Dundalk tomorrow and I'll get a small pair like yours". He tried to persuade me to go to his house a short way down the road where he said his tea would be ready and I could join him and his wife. "You can park up for the night in your tent if you like. You can pick your spot anywhere around the house but we have a spare room you can have with no trouble at all". I thanked him for the offer but explained that it was still early and I wanted to move on as far as I could in view of the fact that I had made an early start for that reason. We shook hands and off he went with his dog and sheep.

In Omeath I talked to a small group of men outside a grocery store and asked about the roads down towards

Ballagan Point area. The general consensus of opinion
was that I would be ok down to just after Ballagan
where they said I should follow the road towards
Petestown to avoid lots of smaller roads that went to the
coast and were just dead ends. I made a note of that plus
the fact that from there, to avoid a maze of minor road, I
would most likely be guided by signs for Dundalk. At
Greenore the wonderful aroma of fish and chips I could
not ignore. I bought three large fish but no chips. I
finished them off in no time and set off again on the
route suggested by the men I had spoken to earlier but
also guided a little by my map which didn't show all the
minor roads but did help with A and B class roads. I
followed the men's quite lucid directions, which I had
recorded, and sure enough after mile upon mile of
narrow roads with very high hedges all the way I
emerged into the outskirts of Dundalk. I did go a bit
astray in a place called Rampark but a young lad of
about 14 on a mountain bike volunteered to get me back
on the main road. He was as good as his word. From
Dundalk I followed the signs to Black Rock and
Lurgangreen then, still following the road along
Dundalk Bay I came to Castlebellingham. Out in the
bay there were at least 20 to 30 sailing boats all heading
out to sea. I assumed they were in some sort of race or
regatta. I liked looking at boats out at sea. I felt we had
something in common in that we both plodded along
steadily.

It had got cold this afternoon and now, early evening,
the headwind from the south east was very strong. I
hoped there wasn't going to be any more hailstone

showers. I had brought with me a soft, quite wide, home-made headband which, in this cold wind I found I could use like a scarf around my neck to keep out the cold. I must admit that as the afternoon had worn on I had felt rather more tired than usual. I thought perhaps that I was really missing my afternoon siestas and should somehow devise a way that I could have a nap, even if only for about 15 to 30 minutes. But now my quest was for an overnight camping place. About half way between Castlebellingham and Anagassan I saw a field some distance away from the road with a high hedges around it. I stopped to consider it but a man passing by directed me to a much better place a bit further on. He said not to go any further along that road as there was a gipsy camp down there. I rode along about a quarter of a mile and there it was. The man said it used to be a camp-site but wasn't used as such any more. "There are toilets there" he said "but I don't think they work". It was perfect for me as far as I was concerned. I had no sooner got there and checked it all out than the man who had spoken to me earlier came to see if I was OK. He introduced himself as Jack Sarsfield. He immediately set about helping me to erect my tent. We then stood chatting until it was quite dark. He went off home and I got on all the warm clothes I had and settled down for the night. I was so tired that I didn't even bother about supper. Anyway, those fish earlier in Greenore had really filled me up.

I was back on the road early, riding along listening to birds singing and rabbits at the side of the road. This was farming countryside with the road keeping close to the sea down to Annagassan. There the it veered inland but soon I came to a side road back towards the sea and Dunany Point where Jack Sarsfield had told me there were some really dramatic cliffs to be seen. I turned seaward at a village called Martinstown and got quite near to Dunany Point but as it involved a trek across fields and paths I decided to carry on towards Dunany and then to Port. Tractors and even a few horses in ploughs were in some of the fields. At Port a postman gave me a great set of directions for the rest of the coast down to Clogher Point. I followed a narrow bumpy and pothole strewn road to a point just short of Hacketts Cross where I re-joined the road down into the town of Clogherhead.

Near the town I came to a long hill where there were some nice tall clean looking nettles on my side of the road in the hedge bottom. My supply of nettles, which I always tried to keep topped up for making nettle tea but also for use in salad sandwiches and in soup, was down to near zero. Here was an opportunity to get myself some really nice looking specimens. I pushed my bike along and kept picking the freshest looking ones here and there as I made my way up the hill and putting them in a plastic bag. As I got to the top of the hill I saw an elderly man leaning over his garden gate watching me. When I got near to him I said, "Hello" but he made no reply. I was about to get on my bike when he said, "Do you mind if I ask you something"? "No" I said, "Carry on". "What have you been picking out of the grass down there? Surely it wasn't all that old rubbish food that people throw out of their cars. People walking their dogs won't even let them near it. You're not eating that stuff are you"? I tried very hard not to laugh at what he had said. I had seen the same rubbish food throw-aways as he had, amongst the nettles. "No" I said, "I have been picking nettles". "Nettles" he exclaimed, "I don't believe you". At this point his wife joined him at the gate. I leant the bike against the fence and took the half full bag of freshly pulled nettles to show him. "And what are you going to do with them"? Was his next question. I told him and added, "You must have heard of nettle tea and nettle soup haven't you?" He made no reply but looked me up and down a few times. "Are you sleeping rough or something? Can't you afford proper tea and proper soup?" I could see his wife was nudging him with her elbow, obviously embarrassed at his line of questioning but I was rather enjoying it. Here I was being taken for a tramp again! At that point I told him what I was doing and that I was spending some nights in a tent but also in hostels and B&Bs. I felt he didn't believe me. He looked at his wife who now had a big smile on her face as much as to say to him, "See, he's not a tramp after all". "What age are you then" he asked and I told him. "Talk to the silly bugger a minute while I come back" he said to his wife and went indoors. "He's a right funny old bugger when you get to know him" she said. "Don't let him upset you with all those questions. He means no harm". At that he reappeared with something fairly large wrapped in a newspaper and tied with string and handed it to me. "Now listen to me" he said, "I don't believe all that stuff you told me about riding your bike all that way at your age. But I can tell you are sleeping rough all right. I've put you some decent food in there so tonight you can eat something proper and not bloody nettles. Throw them away and have some sense at your age. I'm off in now to get a mug of proper tea" and at that he turned and went back into the house before I even had chance to thank him. His wife followed him but before she went she said in a low voice, "I hope he hasn't given you the dog meat. I wouldn't put it past him". I felt that her guess might be correct but I kept the parcel in my hand so that I could look at it somewhere further down the road. When well out of sight of their house I stopped and opened the parcel. It contained a big chunk of fresh cheese still unopened, an unopened packet of dates, plus a tin of beans and one of sausages plus a tin of sardines! There was no dog meat! It was only then that I realised I had left my bag of nettles at his gate where we had been talking. I pondered for a few minutes as to what to do about them. I felt upset at not thanking him at the time for whatever was in the parcel but finished up deciding to keep going.

Thinking about the episode with the man, the nettles and the present he gave me helped keep my mind off my aching wrists'. These rough surfaced side roads were playing havoc with them but instead of really doing something about it I kept telling myself that my wrists would in due course get toughened up to it. From starting out this morning the very strong headwind had not abated. It was so bad that all the time I was forced to stay in the lower gears. It was really made the pedalling hard work. It was so strong that it blew spray from the waves right across the road into the field on the other side of the road. Of course I was getting its full force.

This was quite a new but unwelcome experience. However, the wind seemed to be moving round towards the north. I was hoping it would hurry up as it would then be pushing me along.

Since shortly after setting out this morning I had become aware of a tightness across my chest and some sharp stabbing pains in the region of my heart. I put it down to the effect of the very cold wind which can produce these symptoms in anyone with a dodgy heart condition as I have. I eased off on the pedalling and after about an hour the pains ceased but I was nevertheless a bit worried as it was yet early days into my trip to be having to worry about my health and in particular my heart. In Clogherhead I stopped at a supermarket to get some bottled water and to give myself a break from the pedalling. At the checkout there was a man to whom I had earlier said "Hello" to as I perused the contents of the shelves. When I came out he was standing looking at my bike and asked what I was doing. I explained about my trip around Ireland whereupon he said that I must come and have a cup of tea with him and tell him more about my trip. He lived close by and I needed little persuasion as I was still having a few of the stabbing chest pains and welcomed this distraction. He was a very fit, smart looking man of 60. He introduced himself as Kevin Moore. Over a nice cup of tea and a very tasty sandwich and big piece of cake in his very smart looking house in Oriel Cove he spoke of his life in England and of his fifty years in the Royal Navy. He said he had now been living here in Clogherhead for the past six years. His wife, he said, was helping look after an invalid sister locally. He told me he missed England and in particular the close companionship of workmates for so many years. Of course I told him of my working background and of now being on my own as a widower and could therefore sympathise with him. Two hours just flew past but I felt better for the break from cycling and was extra pleased that my chest ache had gone. It had been an altogether pleasant interlude. About half way to Termonfeckin, I came to a Y junction which wasn't signposted. To ensure that I stayed on the road to Termonfeckin I called at a house on the junction to seek advice. A most beautiful young woman, with a little girl by her side, insisted that I come inside. I joined a salesman who was there selling double glazing. They both gave me the directions I needed. The lady insisted I join them for a cup of tea, which I did, whilst I revelled in the scenic location of the house which was only about fifty yards from the edge of the water. The salesman gave me a new baseball type cap with his firm's logo on it. The lady, a Russian, explained that she was a translator and worked from home on her computer. The headwind had eased off somewhat by the time I had got back on the road. As I neared Termonfeckin my attention was drawn to a sign 'Highfield House. 17th Century Farmhouse. Hostess Kitty McEvoy'. Well that was it! How could I ignore such a coincidence with the name being McEvoy? I got booked in for the night, enjoyed a big evening meal and a great chat with the family who, for the record, were in no way related to my family.

On the outskirts of Termonfeckin there began a series of

'roadside finds' which continued throughout my trip. On the grass verge I saw an almost brand new gents' leather jacket. It obviously hadn't been there very long. From its condition it looked as if it had only been there overnight. I checked all its pockets but there was nothing with which to identify its owner. I hung it on the nearby fence in a very noticeable position in the hope that its owner might pass by and see it. Its position on the grass verge plus the fact that its pockets were empty suggested to me that perhaps it's had been stolen from somewhere during the night, its pockets ransacked, and the jacket itself then dumped by the thief or thieves. A few miles further on I stopped a passing police car going in the direction of where I had left the jacket and told them about it. They said I should have taken it, then reported it and if nobody claimed it I could have kept it. I told them that as I had been dumping clothes since my trip started I wasn't now going to start collecting unwanted clothes, even something as attractive as a new leather jacket. Nevertheless they took my details and said I could enquire about it in a few weeks time as they would now go and take possession of it. I never did enquire about it. I just hoped it got back to its rightful owner in due course.

This morning I had made my mind up that if at all possible I would get through Dublin before the day was over. I followed the road through Baltray then along coast into Drogheda then back down on the other side on the river to Mornington and into Bettystown where I called into the main supermarket in the town centre to get a bottle of water. As I went in through the main entrance I slipped on the smooth wet floor tiles and fell flat on my back. Everyone rushed to my aid, including the staff. It had been my own fault entirely. The Croc rubberised sandals I was wearing have one serious flaw in that they will slip on any smooth wet surface and that was exactly what had happened on this occasion. It had been raining earlier and the floor tiles were wet. Mats were down everywhere but I had managed to step on a place where there wasn't a mat. Fortunately my thick layer of clothing prevented any injury. I thanked my helpers and the staff and truly embarrassed at my own misfortune, made a hasty exit. As I was leaving I overheard a member of staff speaking on his walkie-talkie about the incident. For the first time in my life I heard myself being described as 'an elderly gentleman'. I had never before seen myself in that category of person. At least it sounded more gracious than perhaps being described as 'an old man' which it could well have been. I did my best to ride off in a manner befitting that of an elderly gentleman. Later that evening the extent of the shock I had received in the fall brought it home to me that indeed I was elderly.

From Bettystown I pedalled as quickly as I could through open farmland until I came to Laytown where I had to deviate away from the coast road along a river which brought me up to Julianstown where I crossed the river and made for Balbriggan, Skerries and Rush. In Rush I had a ride out to the pier then doubled back through this very busy little town. From there I rode on to Lusk. This detour inland was such that I felt as if I was going back over where I had already been. On the road to Lusk, at Whitestown, I turned off down towards Rogerstown but found I had to return to the R128 to get around the very unusual looking inland waterway or harbour there. This took me on to the R126 and from there I headed south a little way inland from the coast. In the evening sunlight I spotted Lambay Island just off Portrane. Big white fluffy clouds hung over it. The scene was like that in a beautiful painting. Soon I was in Swords and thus in the outskirts of Dublin. Planes coming and going from Dublin airport flew low overhead and for the first time since I left Belfast I knew I was back in a very busy city. I did deviate a little to the coast line here to have a look at what seemed to be a tiny island just north of Howth Harbour. At Howth Harbour I was looking out at the island with my binoculars and could see what looked like a little castle there but my binoculars weren't powerful enough to see it properly. A young couple, who sounded to be German tourists, standing near me offered me their very powerful binoculars to look at the island. Now I could see a small round tower in great detail but no signs of human habitation. The air around the tower and the huge rock on which it was built was literally crowded in birds of all size and description. On handing the binoculars back to them I learnt that the husband was indeed German but the lady was from Dublin city. She told me so much interesting information about the island, including how it came to be named Ireland's Eye that I seriously thought about staying somewhere close by overnight and tomorrow taking one of the tourist boats out to the island. She showed me a small booklet about the island. I had a quick look through it. She offered to give it to me to read and said I could post it back to her later but I graciously declined her offer. I told her that I was somehow fascinated by offshore islands and maybe sometime I would come back to Ireland and just visit its many islands. This one would definitely be one of them. As we were talking I saw various boats coming and going around the harbour, including two large passenger steamers which could be going to any one of the various English ports.

Now it was into the thick of Dublin's evening rush hour traffic. I had no particular interest in the city itself. I just wanted to get through it safely this evening in the general direction of Dun Laoghaire on its south side. I am quite well acquainted with evening rush hour traffic in most of England's big cities but this was something else. What was new to me was cycling through such traffic. I wasn't prepared for that at all. Other cyclists were zooming past me every second and pedestrians weren't just on footpaths but were dodging through the traffic everywhere. I thought I would be smart and ride in the bus lanes but here I was being hooted at continuously but not by bus drivers but by taxi drivers some of whom passed within inches of me. I had kept to the roads down by the docks once I left the city centre but it seemed that everyone else was doing the same. In the district of Blackrock I saw a Garda station and decided to call in, introduce myself and perhaps while away an hour or so until the rush hour traffic eased off. The reception area was quite busy for that time of evening but after about a fifteen minutes I was approached by a very pleasant young policewoman. She was obviously pleased that I wasn't someone with a problem as such and went off to call a sergeant once she knew I was a retired English policeman just making a social call. Next thing I knew I was ushered into a back office where tea and biscuits appeared as if by magic and a few senior officers came to talk to me. I was asked about my plans for that night's accommodation and when I said I hadn't as yet decided but that I would probably find a place to camp further along the coast that idea was quashed immediately. They insisted I stay in the station overnight and within minutes the furniture in an inner interview room was moved to accommodate me and my panniers etc. My bike was taken around the back into a secure storage area. By this time the afternoon shift were preparing to go off duty. They were on a quick shift change over and would be back again at 6 am.

I made myself scarce for the 10 pm shift changeover by going to a nearby cafe where I had a light meal. I wasn't really hungry as I had been treated to tea, coffee, sandwiches, buns and cake since coming into the station. I went back to the station about an hour later to find the reception area very busy and both duty officers going flat out dealing with all the usual late night problems common to police everywhere. I was let through into the rear office area where I spoke briefly to the night shift sergeant, who was also quite busy and then went to my 'bedroom' where I slept on the floor next to a hot radiator. In the morning I put all the furniture back in its original position and joined the shift from yesterday afternoon. They had brought in all sorts of goodies for me including freshly baked scones. I was taken into the canteen and treated to a Dublin version of Mrs Bree's 'Belfast Breakfast'. I didn't eat all the scones which they had brought in so they were packed up and given to me to have later that day. I was having trouble with one of my mobile 'phones so before I collected my bike I went to a nearby 'phone shop and got the problem sorted out. It was then back to the station, said my farewells and thanks and set off into streets which were thankfully no way as busy as they were the previous evening.

By noon I was down by Dun Laoghaire harbour. Passengers from Holyhead were disembarking from a steamer whilst others passengers were already waiting to go aboard. This was where I initially intended to begin by journey around Ireland but as already stated various influences led to me begin at the Giant's Causeway. I moved along to Dalkey about 2 miles further south. I somehow got lost in a maze of streets in Dalkey I had tried to progress in a southerly direction by keeping along those nearest the sea but that strategy wasn't, for some reason, working. I stopped by a young couple emerging from the gateway to a house and asked if they could direct me towards Bray. They were both in their twenties and can only describe their attire as that of hippies. The reaction I got was totally unexpected. The young woman dashed up to me, threw her arms around me and gave me a great hug followed by a kiss on the cheek. Her companion just stood laughing. I wasn't given any directions to Bray. Instead, holding my left arm, she bombarded me with questions ranging from "Where are you from; where are you going; why are you on your own; where are you staying at night"? I answered that last question first by saying that I had been in a police station at Blackrock overnight. "Wow" she exclaimed, "What had you been up to get locked up? You don't look the type to have been drunk or fighting or on dope". She really had me laughing by this time. Before I could begin to answer any of these questions her friend, who spoke English with a very strong French accent and introduced himself as Ed, suggested I come with them to a cafe at the top of the street where they were going for something to eat. 'Ok" I said, getting off the bike. The girl, who said she was called Enise, linked my left arm and together we all set off up the street towards the cafe. At one point Enise called out to two middle aged couples walking along the street in the opposite direction us. "Hey, this man is famous. He is cycling all the way around Ireland by himself on this bike. He's just got here from the Giant's Causeway up north". I don't think they knew her but nevertheless they came across and we shook hands. After a brief conversation during which Enise and Ed made me out to be some sort of celebrity, the couple went on their way. I got the impression that they thought the three of us had been having something different than porridge for our breakfast! It was harmless fun as far as I was concerned. By the time I had got to the cafe I had answered most of her earlier questions and lots more. I think she was disappointed that I hadn't some wild story to tell them about my all night stay in the police station. The cafe, on a corner, was called Select Stores, Dalkey. It was a store and cafe combined and specialised in what I can only describe as very healthy New Age type food. Enise and Ed recommended various foods and combinations of foods which I had, quite honestly, never experienced before so I settled for the cafe's speciality soup with healthy toasted wholemeal bread. They each chose a healthy vegetarian lunch and together the three of us sat by a window to discuss all our mutual interests. These ranged from literature to art, music, poetry, travelling and psychic matters and much more. Ed, who said he was 26, explained that he came to Ireland in 2001 and had become besotted with Ireland and Dublin in particular. I avoided asking about his obvious friendship with Enise. She said that she had a book of poetry coming out in August. I asked for a sample of her prose and she obliged with the following:

> If all that is, is all there is,
> And there can be no more,
> And if all that is, is all there is,
> Then that's what I adore.

She said her full name was Enise Camara. We were joined at the table by an older lady who was a friend of theirs. I took the opportunity to leave Ed. and Enise and got on my way with only pleasant memories of this most unusual interlude.

This was still a very built up area but after Bray it all changed to more open country and once again I was back near the coast. North of Greystones I met up with a young couple cycling southwards accompanied by two girls aged about 12 or 13. All four were wearing bright coloured cycling clothing plus helmets. Since leaving Dalkey I had seen them a few times but we had just acknowledged each other but here at Greystones I joined them at a road junction. We all pulled over to have a chat. But it became obvious immediately that conversation was going to be limited as they were Polish and spoke very little English. Needless to say I couldn't speak their language. An additional problem was that the batteries on my tape recorder were about to run out. They recorded their names for me but the distortion made it impossible to understand what was being said. The only name I could make out was that of their daughter who was called Lisa. From the conversation we did have I learnt that they lived in Dublin and had come out for a ride together. We had a photographing session then went our separate ways.

North of Wicklow town near Rathnew I got my tent set up where there was a riding school. There were caravans and several horse boxes all parked up. I spoke to the man in charge called George Hernon who reassured me that I would be ok there all night so long as I was away by 9am because that was when the horses would be arriving. I pitched my tent in a place where I thought I would be sheltered but I was wrong. I was awakened at 1.30am by the wind making the tarpaulin flap so wildly that I was sure it was going to be blown away but the long pegs I had got the previous week held tight. This was the second time this had happened so I decided that the next day I would cut the tarpaulin so that one part of it would be for covering the bike and the other for covering the tent. This would mean that it would be easier to stop the part over the tent from flapping in the wind. I would be denying myself the use of the fairly large conservatory-like section in front of the tent which served as a 'dry area' for me before I entered the tent and the same when I got up in the morning if it had been raining overnight. I was now prepared to forgo that luxury in the interests of a good night's sleep.

As the following day was a Sunday I looked forward to a quiet day on the road to Wicklow. On the way I saw a little church with only one car in the car park and decided to go in and say a few prayers. It was empty apart from an elderly lady who had two little girls with her. I had only lit a few candles when there seemed to a lot of activity starting at the back of the church where I had come in. I looked round and saw that people were streaming in. Obviously Mass was about to start so I hurriedly got up and made my way to the door. Only one half of it was open and I simply couldn't get out with the doorway being full of people coming in. I was dressed in my orange waterproof suit and the Crocs without any socks and had my helmet in my hands. I obviously had to wait until this rush of people got in before I could get out so I stood ready by the door. As I reached the door my attention was diverted for a moment or two by a woman standing on a nearby chair putting up notices on a board. I was worried that she might fall. In those few moments, some people passing had put paper money into my upturned helmet. It was only when someone put coins into it that I became aware of what was happening. I couldn't believe it. The people coming in obviously thought I was someone collecting money. Of course my old fashioned round helmet turned upside down would have looked like some sort of collection dish. I almost burst out laughing. At that moment a man had got his purse open ready to put some money in my helmet. I said to him in a nice way, "I'm not collecting money. I'm a cyclist waiting until you all get in so that I can get out". He stood back and looked me up and down, with a long look at my bare feet in my Crocs. "I'm sorry sir" he said. "I thought you were a monk or someone like that doing a collection". I gave him the money from my helmet and asked if he would please return it to the people who had put it in my hat. Now he too was smiling. He was obviously seeing the funny side of it all. He agreed he would return the money to them. "It will be no bother at all" was his response. At that moment there was a lull in the people entering so I thanked the man and got out the door as quickly as I could. So far I had been taken to be a tramp, an explorer, a policeman, a traffic warden and now some sort of poor monk begging for money.

A little further on I stopped to take a photograph of a view over the coastline to include the well-known Wicklow Head, from where I had just come but couldn't find my camera. It took me almost half an hour before I found it in the pocket of a shirt in one of my panniers. As I was doing this I had a bit of a chat with a man cutting a big sloping grass verge with a strimmer. His wife brought him out a mug of tea then, seeing me there, went back inside and brought me one as well, plus a plate of ginger biscuits for us to share. Photograph taken, all biscuits eaten I set off again. For the first time on my trip I saw wind farms, seven of them, some way out off the coast. Their slow turning propellers added to the tranquillity of the whole scene around me as I pedalled along in in glorious sunshine with birds singing everywhere and seagulls gliding to and fro along the cliff tops which dominate this part of the coastline. On the really wide sandy beaches where the waves were rolling gently onto the sand, there were a few people strolling slowly along, some with children and dogs. This was an idyllic Sunday morning scene. The only thing which took the edge off things was the rough condition of the road, particularly the potholes, which I had to ensure I avoided otherwise a buckled wheel could easily be the result. On these rough road surfaces my wrists constantly ached, despite the thick foam rubber sponges I had earlier put on the handlegrips but it was something I hoped would not affect me once this this trip was over. An added problem with the road surface was that when the surfaces were laid it had been done in 20ft sections which somehow left a high ridge at each end so every 20ft I got a double dose of wrist aggravation as both front and back wheels went over each ridge. When I went fast it was almost like riding along a horizontal ladder!

One thing I greatly enjoyed along here was the prevalence of the Whin bushes with their wonderful yellow blooms. This, to me, was a throwback to the memories of my childhood days in the Mourne Mountains where Whin bush hedges were everywhere. I just had to stop and take some photographs of them to keep as a special memory. On a stretch of the road where it dipped down to beach level I was freewheeling along when I saw some brightly coloured clothing in a gateway and stopped to investigate. There were only two items one of which was a duvet. The brightly coloured item was a brand new, single bed size, 'Noddy' blanket. It was lovely and thick, soft and fluffy. Both had been there overnight as they were wet with early morning dew. Firstly I spread them both on the gate then made myself a breakfast as I had only had a small snack earlier in my eagerness to get on the road. I reckoned that if someone had forgotten them they might still come back for them. An hour later, breakfast over and the items on the gate photographed, I was all set to move. Just in case someone camping on the beach had left the items there I had a look along the beach but there was sign of anybody. I decided that I couldn't leave that lovely blanket there to perhaps finish up back on the ground. I rolled up the blanket, now dry, and put it on my rear carrier. I fastened a note to the duvet giving my mobile number, plus the time / date and the fact that I was cycling southwards along the coast with it on the back of my bike. With some mixed feeling about what I was doing I set off southwards once more. If nobody claimed the blanket it would be ideal for me in my tent at night.

Whilst on the subject of items which I have seen abandoned by the roadside I must put left handed gloves top of the list. At the beginning of my journey from The Giants Causeway I had so far counted 27 such gloves but not one was right handed. All were large gloves of the water / oil proof type. The two features of this which intrigued me most were (a) why only left hand gloves and (b) why only on the left hand side of the road when facing south. I could have understood seeing them at laybys where lorry drivers would have stopped to do something to the engine, but not on the grass verges of quite narrow roads. And why only left hand gloves. So far I had only seen one right handed glove. I had not yet seen a right and left hand pair. At this stage of my journey, especially after finding the 'Noddy' blanket, I decided that from now on I would keep a record of things I seen abandoned at the roadside. I realised of course that these observations are the result of cycling over a long distance at a comparatively slow speed with little else to do but observe the surroundings and of course notice anything unusual / different / or special in any other way. It was now going to be a feature of my daily observations. In various places as I went along I mentioned this matter of the gloves to lorry drivers but they couldn't come up with any reasonable solution. Several admitted to throwing two gloves away when they developed holes but not just left handed gloves.

In Arklow I came to the steepest street I had ever seen in any town anywhere. I had to walk up it but stopped at John Joe's Bar where I treated myself to a half pint of Guinness. There were very few people in the place and whilst everyone had a look at me in my unusual attire nobody made any conversation. I wasn't really bothered. I just fancied one of my favourite drinks. When I came out the rain was simply pelting down but I had got so used to rain in all its forms that once I got to the top of the street where the hill levelled off somewhat, I rode on. The one thing I didn't like about walking with my bike was that the rear pannier on my side struck my right leg at every step I took. It was impossible to get the pannier any further back on its carrier so my only options were either walk up closer to the handlebars or walk with the bike at almost an angle of forty five degrees. Both alternatives, in most instances, made it a lot simpler and easier to just stay on the pedals in low gear. Mostly, the only time now that I walked with the bike was on very steep hills. In looking at the contours on my map and listening to information from people who I spoke to along the way, I was going to have to do a lot of walking along the rest of the south coast and certainly up the west coast. Ah well, I might make it back to the Giants Causeway before Christmas!

At the roundabout at the top of the street a signpost showed me Wexford was 69km away. I hoped that by tonight I would have rounded the south east corner of Ireland onto the south coast. South of Arklow I had no alternative but ride on the N11 which to all intents and purposes a motorway with vehicles speeding past covering me in spray. I took a short break under the shelter of an overhead bridge and had a cup of tea from my flask. From there I continued to ride on the footpath most of the way for my personal safety. A few miles after a sign telling me I was now in Wexford I took a left turn down a small road which took me through Killowen Upper and on to Clone Middle then another maze of small coastal roads to Courtown. On the way the rain cleared and in Courtown I stopped for a short rest. After that it was the R142 all along the coast.

On the way I came to a T junction where on my right I saw about half a dozen life sized figures of men and women carved from wood. I stopped to photograph them and met the sculptor, a man in his fifties called Jimmy Kavanagh, who told me that they were all made from lime trees. They were done ever so professionally and in great detail. They were all life size. Several were of men and women standing arm-in-arm or in an embrace. He told me he had some smaller carvings in the yard and in the house but didn't have the time to show them to me as he was rushing to a meeting.

A bit further along the same road, outside a pub called O'Brien's I met a couple, Philomena and Finton, who said they cycled around the Ring Of Kerry about twenty years ago. They raved about its beauty but warned me about the hills I would have to climb. We were joined by quite a few people who came out of the pub carrying their drinks just to see who was this character with the brightly coloured outfit they were talking to. Everybody wished me well. One man seemed intent on going back in to get me a drink to help me on my way but I succeeded in persuading him not to do so. A few miles down the road I came to a memorial stone in a village which was twinned with the town of Serigo in Texas, USA, where during the Famine years about 200 people from that village emigrated to Serigo to begin a new life.

In Blackwater I saw a sign advertising accommodation at 'Inishladhru Farmhouse' and went there. The proprietors Honor and Owen Cash made me welcome for the night in their splendid house up there on the hill from where there was a wonderful view of the countryside. I declined their offer of a full meal but settled for a big plate of various sandwiches and tea. Despite the lateness of the hour Honor put my washing in the machine, including my Noddy blanket. Signs on their walls showed numerous awards they had been granted over the years including The Best Family Home Awards from the year 2000 until the present. When I spoke about them Honor showed me a stack of other awards but explained that she hadn't got around to getting them up on the walls. A local priest called Mike Blake, was there visiting and we had a long talk about everything from politics to history but not religion. He struck me as a very modern 'with it' priest who spoke his mind.

About 11.30pm I was just about to drop off to sleep when I became aware that there was an electricity power cut. I got up and went downstairs with my torches to help but in no time they had various lamps and candles all lit. By the time we had another cup of tea plus a few biscuits the power came back on. The next morning it was breakfast with everything anyone could want to eat but I really fancied the porridge on offer plus Honor's homemade bread. When I was checking my panniers I discovered that somehow water was getting into them despite their waterproof covers. Owen gave me some black bin liners so I put all of my things into them then put the lot into the panniers. Had I more knowledge of cycling with panniers I would have done this before I started out. I shared a breakfast table with a Swedish lady and her German friend. She said they lived in Copenhagan and in Germany but both loved visiting Ireland so much. After breakfast, along with directions for Wexford Town and Rosslare, Honor and Owen gave me a quick input of local history including the fact that this area was the setting for the film Private Ryan some years ago. They also told me that in a nearby village the first signs of the potato blight which later led to the Famine, was discovered. Vinegar Hill, also nearby, was where the Rebellion in 1798 against British Rule began. It was near to lunchtime when I eventually got back on the road again in lovely sunshine and a cool breeze from the very calm sea. It was here that I saw the first thatched cottages of my trip. Of course I had to stop and photograph them.

Eventually I reached Wexford where I walked across the bridge into the town centre then went down to see the harbour. There I met up with a couple strolling along the quay. They were Kevin and Anna Harkin who said they were visiting from Derry for a one week holiday. We chatted for about an hour during which he told me about all the charity walks they do and of his long involvement with getting aid to Bosnia and Romania during the recent wars there. They gave me their address in Derry and invited me to call on them when I reached Donegal. They were such an inspiring couple. Rosslare was to be my next stop. It was a much longer ride than I anticipated from looking at my map. The roughness of the road surfaces was now causing me quite a lot of wrist problems again so I decided it was time to try something other than what I had done over a week ago in Northern Ireland when I lowered the seat and raised the handlebars. At a Texaco Garage I bought two huge yellow car washing sponges to replace the ones I had fitted before. I also bought super glue to make a permanent job of fixing them to the handlegrips. At the same place I bought a roll of masking tape to repair a tear in the tarpaulin. I would have to leave the handlegrips job until I stopped for the night which would give the superglue plenty of time to permanently secure the sponges in place. The previous sponges were only kept in place by insulation tape. All the way from Dublin I had been riding into a strong headwind which affected my throat area mostly. I should have had a scarf for such an eventuality. However, I did have a wide homemade headband which I hadn't used very often so far. I had it to fit across my mouth and nose if I was riding into cold winds which were something I was advised to avoid if possible to prevent angina pains. I don't know why I didn't think of using it sooner. It might have saved me from experiencing the quite severe chest pains I had during the early days of the trip when the winds were much colder than they were now.

I found that the road from Wexford was much better surfaced than the earlier ones further upcountry but was very busy with traffic. I recognised many UK Registration plates on vehicles and assumed most of this traffic was heading, like me, for Rosslare Harbour. I bypassed the town of Rosslare then followed signs to Rosslare Harbour which was to be my furthest point on this south eastern corner of Ireland. There vehicles were everywhere going to and coming from three huge passenger ferries in the harbour. I didn't stay there very long as I wanted to turn my back on the east coast and head west along the south coast. My first south coast town was Bridgetown. I stayed on that road until I got to the R739 where I intended turning south to Kilmore Quay and maybe get a glimpse of the Saltee Islands before dark.

I had only gone a short way along that road when I saw a sign for 'The Hideout'. It was a brown Tourist Board sign. On seeing that unusual name curiosity got the better of me so I turned back to investigate. I followed a very narrow twisty road for a short distance and there it was on the left. It was a pub! I had envisaged a tiny little place as its name suggested but it was in fact quite a large pub with tables outside. The evening had grown cold so the heat inside the pub was most welcome. As it was still fairly early there were only about half a dozen people at the bar. Every head turned when I appeared in my bright red waterproof coat and trousers and equally bright coloured helmet. Now that I had discovered it was a pub I only intended stopping for a quick drink, take a quick look around then be on my way to Kilmore Quay but that was not what fate had in store for me. I took off my waterproof gear while the landlord, Stephen Lawlor, pulled me a pint of Guinness. With all that happened afterwards I never did get around to finding out why the pub was called 'The Hideout'.

I left my Guinness to settle while I went outside to

tighten up the new stand on my bike but found I didn't have the correct size spanner. A man at the bar obviously saw me working at the bike and asked me what the problem was. I told him about my spanner whereupon he went out to his car, got out a huge tool kit and in no time had the stand fixed rock solid. He wouldn't let me buy him a drink and the licensee wouldn't take any payment for the Guinness he had pulled for me. They were impressed when I didn't sample the Guinness until it had well settled as is the tradition of true Guinness drinkers. I'm not one of them but I learnt it from my older brother Johnny a good few years ago when he lived near me in Kilburn in London's 'Little Ireland'. There, in the Irish pubs barmen always kept Guinness 'settling' behind the bar for when the regulars came in and wanted their drink straightaway. The licensee refused to take any payment for my drink saying it was the tradition there that the first Guinness was always free. I didn't believe him but didn't argue. He was just being kind to an obvious 'elderly gentleman'!

Everyone wanted to know all about my trip. Once my glass of Guinness got near half way down another one appeared on the bar in front of me. Now when I went to pay for the drink the licensee said it was already paid for. I decided to keep sipping even more slowly. I asked about the possibility of food and within minutes Stephen's wife Patricia ('Tush' to the locals) served up some specially made soup and home baked bread. She said that was only for a start until she made something else for me. Well, with all the Guinness and the soup and bread I was more than satisfied but next came a big plate of sandwiches. By now the pub was full and I was the only one having food. I knew I was getting drunk even though I tried not to but the atmosphere was wonderful. Any further cycling that evening was definitely out of the question so my thoughts in my now befuddled brain turned to thinking about where I would sleep that night. As everyone had been so impressed by my claim that I had slept in my little tent most nights I stuck to that choice for that night despite offers from the licensee and several of the local people in the bar to accommodate me. Before I fully realised it the time had shot round to well past midnight and I was no longer sober but not yet drunk. One man, whose name was Sean, said his land was just up the road on the other side of the crossroads in a village called Paradise and I was more than welcome to camp there overnight. Well, how could I refuse an offer to camp overnight in Paradise! As I set about preparing to go he wouldn't hear of it. He gave his car keys to a young woman called Rachel Power and asked her to run me up to the field in question in his taxi then bring me back. I accepted but found that the field was further away than I expected but Rachel and I were so busy chatting that I didn't really take much notice of the route, other than it was just after a crossroads junction and that there was a big metal five barred gate into the field. I also noted that next to the gate was a cattle pen and some feeding troughs. I couldn't see into the field in the pitch dark but I wasn't too worried about that. Sean had said there had been cattle in the field but they had been moved a few days previous. Back at the pub there were two more pints of Guinness waiting for me. Now that I had sorted out my overnight accommodation I felt a little more relaxed.

Somehow, over my last two Guinness, I got involved in a discussion about the subject of personal fitness. I decided to have some fun with those present by offering to demonstrate my suppleness by bending down, without putting my hands on the floor, and touching my forehead on the floor. It was a feat of suppleness that had been demonstrated to me in England in 1961 by the then Canadian Log Rolling Champion. I had eventually managed to accomplish it and had practised it regularly ever since but not since I had set out on this journey. That night I felt I could still do it. Firstly I described it and showed how it was done but deliberately did not complete the act. I wanted to tempt others to have a go at it and watch the fun but somehow it must have seemed to daunting for anyone to attempt because nobody had a go at it.

Finally when nobody wanted to try to do it I agreed that I would show them how easy it was. Everyone got out a mobile phone ready to photograph me performing. I gave my camera to one of them, put it on video setting and asked him to take me doing it. How I managed to do it in my drunken state that night has since baffled me but I managed it quite well. I got cheers and claps all round and was persuaded to do it one more time. I did it but only just made it. That final demonstration brought on an almost overwhelming desire to vomit but I managed to overcome it. Now there was even more Guinness on the bar for me but I told Stephen I couldn't possibly drink any more and suggested he distribute them along the bar to the other people. I finished off my last Guinness, put a reasonable amount of cash over the bar and made to leave. I was told I couldn't go until I had shaken hands with everyone there. When that finished my right hand felt as if it had been through a crusher! I got hugs and kisses from all the women and wishes of 'Good Luck' from everyone. The whole pub came out to watch me wobble off on my bike into the darkness. A few of them, obviously too drunk to drive, offered to drive me up to the field in question but I wouldn't let them. Before I set off one of the men whispered to me, "Two of the lads went into the toilets and tried to do what you did and they both fell over. One of them got a right lump on his head and has gone off home without anyone knowing. Nobody but me knows about that yet but I'll tell them when I go back in. God man you were great gas. We'll never forget you". It didn't surprise about the young man falling over in trying to do what I had done as it is not all that easy especially if you have never tried it before of, as was no doubt the case here, the person trying it had also been drinking. I had seen that sort of result many times over the years when I had encouraged other people to 'have a go' at doing it, especially when they had a beer or two. Nevertheless I felt a bit guilty about it but then that, or worse, could as easily have happened to me. I will never forget that night for many reasons but I really did enjoy myself. My worries as I wobbled along the road to the field were that (a) I might not be able to find it in the dark and (b) if and when I did would I be able to put up my tent.

Well, it turned out that my original estimate of how far it was from the pub was not based on doing it in a car as distinct from on my bike. It was a good two miles from the pub but I did find it. It was a big field by the roadside with very long grass. There was a very strong smell of cow manure everywhere but the man did say that he had taken the cows out of the field so I didn't worry on that score but the strong smell of the manure did. Somehow I managed to get the tent together. I locked the bike to a tree in the hedge but for the first time left the panniers on it. I managed to cover my tent with the tarpaulin then crawl inside. Cow manure or no cow manure this was Paradise all right! When I eventually woke up later that morning I was rather surprised and pleased that my head wasn't too sore after all that Guinness. It hadn't rained overnight but the clouds were darkening the clear morning sky and rain was definitely not far off. Shaun arrived to check if I was OK. Satisfied that everything was OK he went off to work and I set about recovering my tent from the cow manure that was ankle deep just where I had put the tent.

Well I certainly learnt one more practical point about camping. Never set up camp anywhere that cows had been grazing recently. There was cow manure everywhere. I had chosen the one place where it was deepest on the ground. It was all over my tent, the tarpaulin, my shoes and clothes. What a mess! I simply got everything together as quick as possible and beat a hasty retreat from Paradise in the direction of Bridgetown. At the pub, around the time I got the sandwiches, I remembered asking Patricia to fill my flask with tea for breakfast but then with all that happened afterwards I had forgotten all about it. As I came down to the pub I thought about calling in to collect the flask of tea to have later but they hadn't opened yet so I carried on.

I was pleased that I hadn't missed Kilmore Quay. It was so pretty in every respect as I rode around it. I saw some seals lying in the sun in one place but by the time I stopped nearby and got my camera some children had disturbed them and they were already back in the water. A little further on I came to a memorial garden set out in memory of people lost at sea. Its main feature was a stone carving of a man with his arms around a young woman. He was consoling her. They were both looking out to sea where the Saltee Islands were clearly visible in the morning sunshine not far offshore. Both figures had very sad expressions on their faces. Nearby was a plaque giving details of the garden's purpose. I was impressed how well it was kept. A bit like the well-kept graveyards one sees everywhere in Ireland. I still didn't feel like breakfast as yet so I went northwards in line with the coast.

It wasn't until I came into a village called Baldwinstown that I realised I had left the R736 road a few miles back. By now I felt hungry but decided that first of all I should rid myself of this pervading smell of cow manure. At a road junction in the town I saw a really wide concrete area where I could spread out my tarpaulin and tent without inconveniencing anyone and wash off the manure. A woman at a nearby house obliged with two big buckets of water and a yard brush. In no time the job was done. I even had to wash my shoes and the pedals and wheels of the bike to get rid of the last of the manure. Apart from one local woman who stopped to ask what I was doing, everyone else walked past as if what I was doing was an everyday occurrence. This woman, whose name I didn't enquire about, said she lived locally but had worked for years as a nurse in Birmingham. We chatted for a little while but I think the smell of the manure got to her and she went but not before wishing me well and good luck. When I finished the job I spread the tent and tarpaulin over a nearby wall and returned the buckets and brush to the kind lady nearby. Now it was time for breakfast. As if by some coincidence I noticed that one of my panniers didn't look as it should. Its lid was higher than it normally was and the fasteners were not secured properly. I opened the pannier to investigate and to my surprise discovered not only my flask full of hot tea but a nicely wrapped feast of sandwiches which would last me all day never mind just breakfast. Now how had that happened I wondered? I was sure that, despite my inebriated state at the pub I would have remembered putting the flask and sandwiches in the pannier, but now I wasn't all that sure. However, the more I thought about it the more I realised that the landlord and his wife were responsible. Somehow unknown to me they had put them in my pannier or got someone else to do it but didn't tell me.

Well, I had a hearty breakfast of delicious 'Hideout'

sandwiches and sweet tea there and then but on the opposite corner of the street as the smell of the cow manure, now in the gutter, was still quite evident. A woman at a house opposite, obviously curious as to my presence, came to her gateway. I gave her my camera and asked her to take my photograph having my breakfast on the corner underneath a signpost festooned with direction signs. When I explained why I had washed my tent etc. she said it was obvious that I wasn't brought up in the countryside otherwise I wouldn't have noticed the smell of the manure. "Sure if you were here in the Spring when the farmers spread it on the fields the whole place reeks with it night and day for weeks". I didn't say anything in reply but I could have told her that I was brought up on a farm in County Down where cow manure was a familiar smell and that where I was now living in England was a huge farming area where the smell of not only cow manure but pig manure is thick in the air in Spring. Breakfast over, tent and tarpaulin dry and all packed away again I once more set off in the general direction of Waterford. It wasn't very long before I was in Wellingtonbridge. My tummy was full, the smell of manure was now only a memory and my head had cleared. I was back on form. On the way to Wellingtonbridge I was joined for about half a mile on a flat stretch of road by three German men on very fancy looking racing type cycles. They were all about 30 years of age, looked very fit and all dressed in professional cycling gear. They told me they had arrived early that morning in Rosslare from Cherbourg and intended cycling 140 kilometres each day on a circular route which would take them back to Rosslare. They said they intended camping out each night in any suitable looking place they could find. At that point I was about to launch into my tale of woe about the cow manure but we were just coming to a steep hill. No way was I going to have the breath to cycle up it at our present speed and tell the tale at the same time. I also realised that they were being sociable in riding with this fellow cyclist but wanted to be on their way. Instead I thanked them for giving me their time and encouraged them to go on ahead. They went up that hill at about three times the speed we had been travelling along the earlier flat stretch. That was the last I saw of them.

From Wellingtonbridge I went southwards to Fethard but decided against going all the way to Hook Head as I would have a long way to double back on the same route. Instead I headed west to the opposite side of the peninsula then back up its coastline to Arthurstown where I caught the ferry across to Passage East. From there I followed a very potholed road along the coast through quaint looking little villages. In a place called Ballyglan I had to come away from the coast a little but finished up in Dunmore East, another town with a very busy harbour. I sat in a cafe by the harbour and enjoyed an ice cream. I listened in to a guide telling this assorted crowd of foreign tourists all about the local history and various attractions. I learnt all about the Tall Ships Race in 2005, the ancient lighthouse and the fishing industry. Later that afternoon they were all going out on a pleasure boat trip around the peninsula but particularly to see the dolphins jumping. From a large scale map in the local tourist office I saw that the south of the peninsula from here westwards was almost all steep cliffs. The coast road was well inland. I followed it through Coxtown, Ballymacaw then north from Corbally to Clougher then to Pickardstown from where I headed south again. It was now dusk so I looked for a suitable camping spot. I called into the Saratoga Bar at Woodstown Strand on the Tramore Road and over a drink asked about any overnight camp sites in the area. The licensee said I was welcome to camp on a large grassed area at the at the side of the pub where there would be no noise to disturb me. He flatly refused my offer to pay for the night's stay. I went out and inspected the camping place and found it to be perfect. The grass was well mown and the ground was level and dry. There were thick hedges on two sides of the grass area with one side open down onto a sandy beach. Swings and slides indicated that this was a play area for patrons' children. I set up my tent in a well sheltered corner. As I was doing this I saw two men dressed in bright yellow waterproof clothing and wellingtons out in the shallow surf collecting something with rakes and putting whatever it was in plastic bags. I was intrigued by this and just before I went back into the bar they came past me. They both had identification badges hung around their necks. I asked them if they would satisfy my curiosity by telling me what they were collecting. They told me they were from the Ministry of Food and were collecting samples of mussels to be examined for any signs of disease. They didn't elaborate and off they went.

I had a few drinks and sandwiches. I would save what was left of my other sandwiches for breakfast. I went and sat at a table where a middle aged man was sitting alone. He wasn't very talkative but did tell me that he was German and lived locally. He asked me if I was a tourist. When I explained what I was doing he said he had once travelled around Scotland in a horse and cart and at night slept under the cart. He told me that he was in the process of divorcing his fifth wife then, as if that reminded him of something he needed to do urgently, he got up and walked out of the pub without even saying goodnight. I sort of wondered if the smell of the cow manure was somehow still on me. Maybe I should stock up on better deodorant! However, some locals, who said they knew the man, asked me to join them. With them the 'craic' was great and I was disappointed when closing time came. One couple in the group, who lived nearby, tried hard to persuade me to have a room at their house but out of courtesy to the licensee I tactfully declined their offer. I collected my two mobiles, which the licensee had kindly been charging up for me and headed for my tent, which I had earlier gone out and set up. This was a lesson from the previous night's experience when I had to set the tent up when I was in no fit state to do it properly. In a way I felt I was getting like one of those travelling monks of olden times in Eastern countries who travelled about living for free on the kindness of people. This was a new life experience for me.

I was wakened just after 6am by the sound of tractors nearby and on looking out saw what I took to be about twenty or more men down on the beach with the tractors. Some of the tractors were actually quite far into the tide. They also had several high sided trucks with them and appeared to be on some sort of beach clearance operation. I ignored them and decided to get moving as it was another nice sunny morning. Whilst I was doing this two vans and a few cars parked up nearby and men whom I recognised from their northern Europe accents as Polish joined the men on the beach. I asked a woman passing by with her dog about all this activity. She told me that the men on the beach were all Polish from a very large factory in Tramore which processed mussels and sent them all over Ireland and throughout the world. Now I understood why the Ministry men were there last night. Later as I cycled towards Tramore the high sided lorries I had seen earlier on the beach, plus the various vans and cars passed me in convoy. The lorries were laden to capacity with what looked like seaweed but was no doubt mostly mussels.

The weather had changed considerably in the short time since my journey began. Now, on the south coast it was much warmer every day. In the interests of my own safety on the roads I continued to wear my bright orange coloured waterproof suit but now I had taken to rolling the trouser legs up to my knees. All I wore underneath was a pair of underpants and of course on my feet the Crocs without socks. In planning my trip around Ireland I had thought about camping every night by the sea. In doing that I could easily get washed in the sea. Well the washing side of my plan hadn't worked out so I relied on stopping off at rivers and streams on my route but now I was thinking of revising that plan. I decided that if I could from now on I would stay in hostels. That seemed much more sensible. This would mean I would meet up with likeminded people and in the late evenings would have company and of course I could cook my meals properly and rely less on sandwiches. I had cooking facilities with me in the form of a miniature gas primus stove plus a multi-purpose pan but I hadn't so far seen the need to use them. I had even thought about dumping them at one stage. As for hostels; well I had never stayed in one but perhaps now was an opportunity to have that new experience.

For about a week now I hadn't felt my usual healthy self. Apart from those two occasions when I had more beer to drink than I should, I felt unusually tired and listless. I felt that somehow I was ill but couldn't pinpoint the reason. As I headed for Tramore that was exactly how I felt as I began facing into the steepest hills I had experienced so far. That morning I hadn't had a breakfast as such, just a bottle of milk and one sandwich. Twice this morning I had walked up hills that up to now I wouldn't have done. After about the third such hill I stopped at the top of it and decided to have a rest by the side of the road on a wide grass verge and then have something to eat. It was after all almost lunchtime. I put the bike on its stand and sat down on the grass with my back against the fence. I had no intention of going to sleep but that was exactly what happened as soon as I had sat down. I awoke about 45 minutes later but felt better for the rest. There was very little traffic on this stretch of road so maybe that was why I managed to sleep so long. I sat there musing about how I must have looked to anyone passing. If I

had slipped down to one side I might have caused undue
to alarm to someone passing who might have thought I
had collapsed, or worse! As I sat there I found myself
watching a big black beetle a few feet away. It was
struggling to make its way through the long grass
towards the narrow strip of loose gravel at the side of
the road. Every six inches or so it stopped for a rest then
pushed on. I thought that maybe I should take a lesson
from its approach to tiredness. I watched it until it
reached the gravel where it then made for the edge of
the tarmac, no doubt intending to cross the road where it
would be very lucky if it wasn't squashed by a passing
vehicle. At the edge of the gravel where the tarmac
began, it stopped. It made various little movements of
its body every few minutes which, I thought, were
similar to a person looking both ways before crossing.
But it didn't make any effort to carry on across the road.
One of my hobbies is entomology, the study of insects,
so the longer the beetle dallied by the roadside the more
interested in it I became. It made no attempt to move to
either side or turn back when a few cars went past.
Altogether it stayed in that position for almost fifteen
minutes by which time I was totally baffled as to why it
didn't set off across the road. Then I asked myself why
was I waiting to see this harmless insect getting
squashed on the road instead of doing something to help
it as I would want someone to do if I was in that
position. At that I broke off a large leaf from a nearby
docken and put it in front of the beetle. It immediately
clambered onto it then stopped. I carried both across the
road and set the leaf down in the grass near the hedge
and as soon as I put the leaf down, the insect, which
hadn't moved since I picked it up now casually,

119

scrambled off the leaf into the even longer grass and carried on into the hedge. I went back to my bike and rode off deep in thought about what I had just seen and done. Maybe it was only the life of a little insect but at least I had possibly extended its lifespan for a little while longer. I can recall quite a few incidents in my life where just that same sort of action saved my life. I even wondered if somehow it was an omen of some sort. Maybe someday I will discover the answer to that beetle's behaviour.

As I set off I felt much better for my little rest. This stretch of coastline was most spectacular for its cliffs and panoramic views out to sea. Near Tramore I met up with a Mr Pat McCormack having a break for the moment from driving his car which was parked nearby. I was looking for information about the road to Dungarvan including directions. As well as giving me the directions he went on to inform me that this stretch of coastline was known as the Copper Coast. Here was the place in the whole of the British Isles where copper was first discovered. For some reason the authorities kept the discovery secret for many years. Apparently the next place copper was discovered was in Canada then in America many years later. Not only copper was produced here but also tin. Near where we stood he pointed out a museum dedicated to the history of copper mining in the area. An ancient mine shaft is part of the museum and visitors can be taken down into it with a guide. I saw a group of men doing something with some sort of equipment outside the mining museum and went over to investigate. They were amateur radio enthusiasts setting up their equipment in preparation for contact with other amateur radio enthusiasts at other copper mines throughout the world later that day. I enjoyed a long and fruitful conversation with the men as I too shared an interest in the same hobby many years ago. They suggested I camp nearby and stay with them overnight and take part in their event. It was going to be a 24 hour session with refreshments laid on. I was so tempted to stay but as in a good few other instances over the past few weeks I reluctantly decided to move on. In this instance the main reason why I decided not to stay was that I still didn't fell too well and was a bit concerned that I was perhaps going to be ill. That night I didn't want to be camping out.

By mid-afternoon I was in Tramore, very tired and weak. As I got closer to the town I had begun to feel desperately thirsty. For the first time I now had a clue as to what was troubling me. I must be suffering from dehydration. Apart from the beer I had over the past few days I had drank no water, only what was in the few cups of tea. From Dundalk down I had been drinking mainly bottles of milk and never thought about the importance of drinking water as well. I chose the milk because of its vitamins, etc. I had now learnt another valuable lesson! I went into the Sea Horse Cafe in Strand Street, Tramore, where I ordered a big pot of tea plus a few buns. In ten minutes I had polished off the tea and the buns and within the next forty five minutes or so I had drunk another three teapots of tea and another half dozen buns. Already I felt so much better. I explained to the two staff, namely the waiter Phillip and waitress

Ronnie, what I thought was the matter with me. As a result the proprietor Chris Connolly, came to make sure I was ok. A party of six American tourists who were at a nearby table came to talk to me as they too were keen cyclists in The Florida area and wanted to know all about what I was doing and why. I was photographed with the group who then gave me various email addresses so that we could be in touch later. I then had a problem trying to pay for everything I had eaten and drank. I eventually was allowed to make a contribution to the price but only under strong protest from Chris Connolly. Within half an hour of leaving the cafe I cycled up a really steep hill with no problem at all. I now felt back on form and resolved to keep up my intake of water from now on.

Outside Tramore I asked for some directions from Mr and Mrs Connor who lived locally, who were walking along the road with their little boy Daragh. After they gave me the directions we had a conversation during which I discovered they were familiar with parts of Alaska where I had been travelling recently. Daragh was riding a childs' bike which I noticed didn't have a bell so I took the opportunity to give him the one I had been carrying in a pannier since I started but had never got around to fitting it to the handlebars so I gave it to him as a surprise present. His parents said they would keep it as a souvenir of their meeting up with me.

Next I was back on the beautiful wide open countryside along the Copper Coast that led me down to Annestown.

On the way there I took a photograph of a brightly painted old time hand water pump. I hadn't seen one of those for years. However, I was going to see many more before this trip was over.

It was getting dusk as I arrived in Bunmahon. On the approach to the town I saw a B&B sign for 'Copperfield House'. The sign was pointing up a long steep hill which was so steep that I knew I would have to walk. The sign also stated: 'Take first turn on the left'. From where I was I couldn't see any left turn so I guessed it had to be at the top of the hill somewhere. A man and woman were approaching me down the hill so I asked them how far away the left turn was. They didn't know as they hadn't been to the top of the hill but as their car was parked close they said they would drive up the hill and check where it was. Although I said not to worry, I would walk on up to see the accommodation, they got in their car and drove off up the hill. In minutes they were back and told me where it was so I kept on walking. It took me about fifteen minutes but when I got there the proprietor very apologetically told me there were no vacancies. As I turned back to the gateway of his house the couple whom I had just spoken to were there in their car. They said they had come back to see if I had got a room and if not they knew of a place that would have a room. I told them what the man had said. They said they would take me in their car to the other B&B. The proprietor was watching from his doorway and I told him of the couple's offer and asked if I could leave my bike with him overnight, minus the panniers. He readily agreed and helped me take it around the back. I took the panniers and joined the couple in the car. Apparently they had already telephoned this other place and there was accommodation available for me. This second B&B was called 'Carrie's At Carrigcastle'. I was introduced to Carol Anne Wilkins the proprietor and installed in my room. The couple who had been so helpful were Jim Nolan and Trudy Hartley of Kilmoylan near Waterford. From the lady at the B&B I learnt that Jim is a very well-known Irish playwright.

I didn't sleep very well during the night due an upset stomach which was, I think, was an after effect of my recent bout of dehydration. This led me to leave a note at 5 a.m. for Mrs Wilkins that I wouldn't be having breakfast. Instead of having breakfast she took me in her car back to the first B&B where I collected my panniers and got on my way. I felt a lot better once I started cycling. However, before I left Bunmahon I called into 'Kennedys Grocery and Drapery' where I bought a packet of needles and some thread to repair a hole which had developed in my jacket pocket. Apart from grocery and drapery the proprietor, Pamela Fenton, ran a very successful cafe on the same premises. Now I was ready for breakfast. I had tea and two large baguettes of salad and ham followed by a few buns. All trace of my upset stomach, or whatever it was, had gone. I rode on until I came to Youghal from where I telephoned my friend John Lawlor. His son Liam collected me and I spent that night and the following two days with the Lawlor family who had been my friends over of many years when we both lived near each other in Yorkshire. Over these few days John gave me an intensive history tour of the whole Cork area including the museum devoted to The Great Famine and the people who sailed to America from there during those terrible years. On the afternoon of the 23rd May I was back on the road. I was now wearing a new pair of real leather gloves, especially designed for cyclists, which John gave me.

I took the ferry, just south of Cork City in mid-afternoon and made for Kinsale along a maze of small twisty coastal roads past Carrigaline and then Belgooley. I didn't stop in Kinsale but rode on along the various narrow twisty roads back towards the coast. There was a vicious cold headwind despite a clear sky and sunshine. I avoided the end of the Ballymackean peninsula. I wanted to make use of what daylight I could. Overnight I had been thinking about my overall progress. Whilst I was pleased with it I was now beginning think from what people had been telling me about the ruggedness of the west coast that I had a tough time ahead of me where I would need to make the most of every day in terms of mileage.

Near Ballinspittle I spoke to a couple who were doing something to their front garden and asked about a place to camp overnight. Without any hesitation they offered me a place in their field by the house. I said I wanted to pay for the pitch but they wouldn't hear of it. Their little girl was with them so I found a solution by giving her four Euros 'for her money box'.

As I rode near Ballinspittle the next day I saw a sign: "Grotto" with an arrow pointing up a steep hill to my right. A few years ago I had heard so much about a statue of the Virgin Mary in Ballinspittle which was seen to move. I didn't know if this was the same one or not but as two women were standing talking near the sign I asked if it was the same statue. They said that they thought it was and directed me to go up the hill and turn left and I would find it. I asked if it was far and they said it wasn't so off I went but had to walk as the hill was very steep. It took about fifteen minutes to get to the left turn and another ten minutes cycling on a lesser hill but there was no sign of a grotto. A farmer on a tractor in a field at the top of this hill told me I was on the wrong road. I should be up the next left. I told him what the women had told me and then added, rather foolishly, "This statue doesn't keep changing places does it"? He gave me a long hard sour look, turned his back on me and drove off. I knew he didn't see the funny side of my comment. I cycled back to where I had turned off and carried on up the hill to the next left where, sure enough, there was another "Grotto" sign and within minutes I was at the grotto. It was beautifully laid out with flowers everywhere. I assumed it was the grotto in question.

At the same time as I arrived a car with four occupants parked up. A young couple and an elderly couple got out and joined me. They too had come to see the statue for the first time and confirmed that it was the one in question that was alleged to have moved whilst someone was praying in front of it. The young couple had a camera and were taking a series of photographs so I volunteered to take one of them all together with their camera. They agreed and got lined up in front of the statue for me to take it. I suggested that they should move more to their left. I wanted to have a full view of the statue as well as them rather than them obscuring the statue but didn't explain why I had asked them to move. As I suggested they move to the left the young man said, "I think you should ask the Virgin Mary to move. She's good at that". He got stares from the other three. I smiled as I knew just how he felt. I took the photograph of the four of them. I didn't dare as do the usual, "Smile please". Their serious faces more than equalled that of the face of the Virgin Mary. I then left. Not another word had been spoken but I imagined that if the statue could have smiled it would have done so.

For the past two weeks I had become accustomed to seeing election posters everywhere but only one attracted me. That was one of a candidate called Sinead Sheppard who was seeking election in the Cork area. She looked like a film star and her smile was something special. I actually looked forward to seeing her posters as I rode along. I would have liked to have had one as a momento of my trip but didn't dare take one. I was really going to miss her lovely smile when I left her area.

After a hard morning's ride over ever increasing hills I felt it was time for a proper Sunday lunch. I had one in The Pink Elephant Bar and Restaurant, at Harbour View,

Kilbrittain. As I went in I thought there must be some sort of tractor rally at this place as there were vintage tractors parked everywhere but there was nobody with them. There were a few cars amongst them but most of the cars were parked on the approach road. As I went inside there was some sort of commotion going on. The place was packed with men who were obviously the tractor drivers but some of them were shouting at a member of staff about something. The next thing happened was that the men all walked out, some of them leaving their meals on the tables. I decided not to order anything to eat in case there was some problem with the food. Instead I bought a drink and waited to see what the problem was. I heard all the tractors starting up and through the window saw most of them leaving. This was interesting. After a few minutes all the tractor drivers returned and sat back at their tables. I went to the door and looked outside and saw that all the tractors had now been moved from the car park onto a large nearby grassed area and cars were now parking in the car park. I asked a member of staff at the bar what the problem had been. He said the tractor drivers had all parked in the car park and car drivers were having to park on the road. Apparently if the tractor drivers had given advance notice of their intention their parking requirements could easily have been catered for thus avoiding all the fuss. I ordered my meal and enjoyed it at a table outside in the company of some of the tractor drivers. They were happy enough about it all as the management had said all of the drivers, including the car drivers, could have a free coffee or tea after their meal as a token of good will.

After the meal I got on my way. Near to a village called Courtmacksherry on the Timoleague to Clonakilty road I found a ladies handbag. It was a small one and contained cash, credit cards, passport and other personal effects. The details on the cards etc. showed that the owner was a Lauren Elisabeth Weiler with an address in Vancouver, Canada. Moments later a few cars passed by. I was sure that had I not found the purse it would have been flattened by those vehicles on this narrow road as it had been lying in the car tracks. As it was I had recovered her purse intact. As it was obvious that it had perhaps been lost in the past half hour or so I fastened it to the handlebars of the bike and rode on. I hoped that the loser might return to look for it but would see it hanging on my handlebars. That didn't happen. In Timoleague I found a Garda station which was actually a house where a Garda officer lived but there was nobody there. There was a telephone handset in the door which gave me immediate access to an officer at the main station in Skibbereen. The officer asked me to put the handbag and my details through the letterbox and it would be attended to when the local Garda officer came on duty at 6pm that evening. I was reassured that if the loser contacted any Garda station in the country they would be informed that the purse had been found. They would also be given my details. From finding the purse to informing the Garda   took up a lot of my time. However, I was happy that had found it and even more happy to know that in a roundabout way I had helped a Canadian. Why? Because when I toured Canada and Alaska shortly before my Ireland trip the Canadian people were so kind and helpful to me.

Outside Clonakilty I took the road south back towards the coast. Some men constructing a new gateway at the roadside assured me that it would take me along the coast 'for a good bit' but I would have to come back to the main road to get to Skibbereen. He said I would be safer to be off the main road anyway as it would very soon be full of traffic coming back from a weekend commemoration to victims of the Famine. It was a pleasant but very hilly road which took me much longer than I expected. In Ross Carbery I stopped at a small store cum petrol station to ask about any hostels nearby or campsites. I enquired from a woman who was getting out of a car nearby. By coincidence she was on the management of the nearby Celtic Ross Hotel and offered me accommodation there at a price I could not argue about. She was Margaret O'Driscoll. I went there and was given a big room with the luxuries of the top class hotel that it was. I did my washing and put my things to dry on the radiators and went down to tea. After a lovely meal I watched television and had a chat with some other guests but by 11pm I was in bed asleep. On such occasions as these I sometimes wondered why I had subjected myself to the various hardships of sleeping in a tent when I could easily have treated myself to more home comforts. My conclusion always was the same; the tent experience was more of a challenge as was the act of cycling around Ireland rather than using any one of a number of other modes of transport. However, with camping as I was doing I was missing the company of people in the evenings, hence my decision the previous week to find hostels to stay in. There I would no doubt find other travellers and enjoy their company and do my own cooking and washing.

The next day was the first time on my trip that I experienced thick fog. It came in off the sea but cleared up by early afternoon. On the N71 road I was overtaken by a middle aged woman on a bicycle who enquired what was I doing? When I told her she said there were many beautiful and interesting side roads to be experienced nearby instead of cycling on the main road and offered to take me along one of them which would also shorten my distance to Skibbereen. I took her up on her offer. It turned out to be not much more than a track but certainly came under the heading of 'interesting'. She described all sorts of trees, shrubs, flowers and much more as we went along for about a mile or so. We crossed streams and had to walk up steep slopes where for certain nobody had been in a vehicle for some time as the 'road' was overgrown with grass. Had it been a man who had taken me on this diversion I would have been worried and thinking about the possibly of being attacked in one form or another. Eventually she stopped by a gateway to another steep laneway which she said led to her cottage away up on the hill. During our ride together I learnt that she is a native of Devon and has lived in in various parts of the UK including Selby, East Yorkshire, which is near to where I live. She produces DVDs on a host of subjects which can be viewed on her several websites under www.gillianknebel.com I was so pleased that she shared this short time with me on the road. What an interesting woman to meet anywhere let alone on this lonely road in West Cork! There we parted and I set off up a very steep track to the top of a hill from where I saw in the distance not only Skibbereen but a number of lakes and even the sea. Eventually this rough road led me into the outskirts of the town which was crowded out with cars and people as I had been warned it would. I carried on through the town in the hope of making it to Mizen Head, the most southerly part of Ireland.

It was tough going on the many very steep hills. I knew I was unlikely to make Mizen Head before nightfall so called at a total of five B&Bs along the road but they were all full. Whilst doing this I got a 'phone call from the Garda officer at whose house I had left the Canadian woman's purse. During the afternoon she had gone into Bandon Police Station to check if anyone had found her purse and was overjoyed to find that it had been recovered intact. That made my day.

Having no success with accommodation I asked a man at a roadside house in the village of Toormore, on the road to Mizen Head, if he knew of any campsites locally. After a short chat he insisted that I pitch my tent in his front garden. I accepted and set up my outfit in one corner of the garden where I wouldn't do any damage to the flowers or shrubs. I was going to cut my tarpaulin into two pieces, as described earlier, but decided to leave it until tomorrow. The man said he would be going to work about 6am in the morning and apologised in advance if he would disturb me when he started up his lorry. He added that according to the local weather forecast the next day was going to be fine. I had a quick supper of sardines and got settled down for the night.

I awoke just after daylight following a disturbing dream in which I heard three youths talking close to my tent. I had heard one of them saying, "There is someone under the tarpaulin" and started pulling at it whereupon I had started shouting and swearing at them. In my dream I then came out from under my tarpaulin and the three of them ran off but I caught one of them as he climbed over the garden wall onto the road. I pulled him to the ground then pushed his head under the water in a small pool nearby until he stopped struggling. I let go of him and looked to see where the other two had gone but there was no sign of them. The youth I had attacked got to his feet, climbed over the wall and went off down the road. That was when I woke up. What a disturbing realistic dream! As I got packed up I decided that in future I wouldn't camp in sight of a road again. I even began to think that maybe it was some sort of omen for me to act upon. That sort of scenario had never crossed my mind before. In preparing for my journey I had made plans as to what I would do in such an eventuality as I had described but those plans bore no resemblance to that dream. Altogether it had greatly disturbed me. Before I left I put a 'Thank You' note through the man's letterbox plus and amount of cash which I knew was roughly the same as a one night campsite fee.

I found the countryside on the way to Mizen Head quite barren with little isolated cottages dotted about on the hillsides. Quite near to Mizen Head I came to a T junction which didn't have a direction sign for Mizen Head so I took a chance on turning to my left. With a powerful wind behind me I went about 2 miles down that road when I began to wonder if this was the road to Mizen Head. A man I asked directed me back to the T junction and said to keep going straight ahead as Mizen Head was about seven kilometres further on. I turned back, now facing into the very strong wind only to find that there were no less than three signs giving direction to Mizen Head. Of course I hadn't looked at them as I passed as the signs were then facing away from me so all I would see was the back of them! To say that I was annoyed would be to put it mildly! As I rode on I came to a brown Tourist Board sign stating that Mizen Head was 3 km away. However, right beside it was a white road sign pointing to Mizen Head. The numbers on the sign showing the distance in kilometres had been removed but their outline was clearly visible. They showed the distance as 7 km. Now I had it figured out. The sign I was now looking at had obviously been taken from the T junction further back and put here, with its numbers removed. I photographed both signs. I think someone should explain to whoever is in charge of such signs that they are meant for visitors like me who are not sure of where they are going and need help from properly thought out sign positions. Mizen Head Tourist Board complex was excellent with its clean modern cafe which had a wide range of food on offer. As for its Information Centre, you could easily spend most of a day in there. I celebrated my achievement at reaching this point with soup and sandwiches followed by a few hours relaxation in the Information Centre and outside chatting with other visitors until somewhere about 5pm when I set off northwards towards Bantry. I was looking forward to seeing the West Coast, in particular the Galway area which was where my mother was born.

Just beyond Toormore I saw a large grassed area by the roadside. Large uncut stones were sticking out of the ground, all at about the same height and quite close together. The surrounding fields had no such set up. My guess that this was a graveyard from Famine times was confirmed by the occupants of a car with Irish registration plates which stopped nearby. The occupants, two elderly men and two equally elderly women, got out carrying flowers and went into the graveyard and put them by one of the stones. They stood there a long while in silence then making the sign of the Cross they walked back to their car. They were all visibly upset in particular one woman who was openly crying. They drove off slowly. I too continued on my way very much affected by not only the people but the whole thought of the Famine times in this and other areas of the country.

A few miles from Durrus on the Mizen Peninsula on the R591 I saw a sign to Dunbeacon Campsite. The proprietor, Kiera, said she would certainly charge up my two mobiles overnight. There was quite a slope on the pitch but I found a level spot down near the entrance and set my tent up there. However, when I went back up to the house to give my mobiles to Kiera, I spotted a much better place to pitch my tent. It was right on the top of the hill near to where two other tents so I brought my tent up there. I didn't really know why I preferred the second pitch. I think it was that I didn't feel too safe down by the entrance from the road. I put that feeling down to the disturbing dream I had last night. The fee was six Euros which was an enormous saving compared to what I had been paying at the B&Bs on my way to here. She also gave me two campsite guidebooks which covered my routes northwards.

In planning various aspects of this trip I dreamt up some new ideas. One was the use the tarpaulin as I had been doing. The second was to carry a sack and each night fill it with grass to make a pillow. Well, this was my first night with a sack full of grass. On this night I cut my tarpaulin into two parts. One to cover the tent and the other the bike. Well, about 2am I was awakened by the heaviest rain I had experienced so far. I managed to get back to sleep about 3am and didn't wake up until almost 7am to find that the rain was still lashing down. The weather forecast last night on my radio did mention it but I hadn't taken much notice. For the first time I used my cooker and made some porridge and then tea and toast then went back to sleep until almost 10am. So far on my trip I had never slept like this. It was 11am when I next awoke. It was still raining but not just as hard. The weather forecast stated it would be raining all day. I would have to stay here a second I night so I went across to the house to tell Kiera then set off to a nearby shop to get some food. I spoke briefly with two other campers, both of whom were packing up to move despite the rain. Both were experienced campers and said that you should never let rain influence you. It always brightens up afterwards they said. At that stage I had mixed feelings about their logic and carried on. Down by the entrance I saw that the pitch where I was going to stay last night was now under about 9" of rainwater. I was now so pleased about my decision. No doubt the experienced campers had decided to pitch where they did rather than down near the entrance where it was on the flat and thus exposed to rainwater from up on the hill. I reckoned that I was beginning to learn a few things about camping.

At that point I decided that I too would move now and went back and packed up my tent, told the lady of my change of mind, collected my mobiles and set off. It was about 2pm and the rain had definitely eased off. I was pleased with my decision to move on. In a charity shop in Durrus I bought a lightweight pair of trousers for 2Euros. They were similar to the pair I had abandoned at the start of this trip except that they didn't have zips at the knees. I felt I needed them as an alternative to my waterproofs and the very few other items of clothing I had if I was going to be staying on campsites and in hostels. I was also pleased to learn there that I had lost four inches off my waist size since I had started out. From Durrus I rode around the fairly small peninsula called Sheeps Head. What a wild desolate place that was but the scenery was breath taking in its beauty. The only few people I saw were car drivers. By teatime I was back in Bantry, the place which features in so many Irish ballads, where I had a quick cup of tea in a cafe the rode on to see how far around the Beara Peninsula I could get before dark. From my maps I saw that this peninsula and the following two, namely Iveragh Peninsula and Dingle Peninsula, were all mountainous. I reckoned it was going to be an endurance test. At Bantry the rain stopped and the sun shone once more, so on my way towards Glengarriff I took several photographs of Bantry Bay bathed in sunlight. Many different types of

small boats, some with sails, were in the bay.
Everywhere along here there were signs of life on the
move. My only problem was a very strong wind coming
in from the Atlantic.

In Glengarriff I stopped at a small, interesting looking,
shop and cafe combined. Its name was The Black Cat
Shop And Cafe. I had the usual cup of tea during which
the couple who own the place asked me all about my
journey. Somehow during the conversation with the
couple the problem with midges came up during which I
showed them the midge net which was part of my Tilley
Hat. The man said there was a much more efficient type
of midge net, namely the thigh part of a woman's nylon
stocking. The stocking should be cut just below the knee
and a knotted there. The top of the stocking could then
be pulled down over the head and neck to form the
perfect net. He said that he and others regularly used
that system in any situation where midges were a
problem such as when cutting turf on the bogs. I thought
it was an excellent idea and bought a pair of ladies'
tights there and then. He got scissors and in no time I
was kitted out with two very efficient midge nets. Of
course the camera had to be brought into action to
record this moment.

By the doorway I saw a large number of the most
unusual looking walking sticks I had ever seen. They
were of all shapes and sizes and mostly all shiny black
colour, like blackthorn sticks. I have had a lifelong
interest in walking sticks and have made some for

people over the years but they were nothing as professional looking as these. At that point their maker, Joe Denis O'Shea came from the back of the shop and a lengthy conversation ensued during which I learnt all about his many years' experience of making walking sticks and of how tourists from all over the world bought them. He and I were still talking when the shop closed for the evening. I got some advice from them about the nearest campsite, which was in fact only a short distance away on the outskirts of the town. I went there, got booked in and set up my tent then came back as Joe had requested. By this time it was dark but Joe was waiting for me. At that point I learnt that he was eighty six years of age! He looked no more than sixty and was extremely fit. He put it down to being a hard worker all his life and to having a positive attitude to everything. We got in his car and set off out of the town a good few miles where we stopped by an area of thick woodland where he said he was going to show me how he selected the wood for his sticks. Well, he had me jumping across a stream at one point and pushing my way through bushes and briars and shrubs of all sorts to a place where he cut most of his sticks. He cut a few sticks and then some special types of fine twigs and demonstrated how he made them into the sticks I saw in the shop. I deliberately won't elaborate here on the methods he uses to finish off the walking sticks to the standard which are for sale in the shop. It was almost midnight when we got back to his shop and I went off to my tent and bed. What an altogether interesting evening I had that evening in Glengarriff.

The following morning, about five miles south of Glengarriff, at the top of a steep hill, I saw a sign at a house by the side of the road: 'GLENGARRIFF HOME BREW CENTRE'. Well this I couldn't pass up. Many years ago I had been an enthusiastic brewer of both beer and wine and was interested to see how it was being done here and of course maybe getting to sampling some. After all I wasn't driving a car so it wouldn't be against the law. There was no reply to my knocking on the house door. A handwritten note on the door said, "If no reply then shout, hoot or yell". I saw that there was a key in the lock so I could have opened the door and gone in but I didn't. I went around to the back where there was a small yard and shouted "Hello" several times and as loud as I could but still got no response. The whole place looked rather shabby and run down, particularly around the back. However, I felt a little uneasy about what I might find if I persisted so I got back on my bike and rode on.

In Adrigole I had stopped at a shop when about half a dozen motorcyclists pulled in after me and asked for directions to Dursey Island. They consulted my map and found it to be off the end of this peninsula. They bought me a coffee and we had long chat about our joint experiences of travelling in Ireland. They were experienced campers who had travelled as a group all over Europe and even in the USA. I learnt a lot from them about the practical side of camping. None of them had ever cycled alone and camped alone like I was doing and thought it to be a most unsafe thing to do. They encouraged me to stick with campsites and hostels. They were making their way northwards up the west coast and hoped that we would meet again somewhere along the way.

I was now really into some of the steepest hills I had as yet experienced. These were the foothills of the Caha Mountains. To add to my difficulty the gears started playing up. Finally I had to stop and spent almost an hour adjusting them then it was off again up and down more steep coastal hills, this time the foothills of the Miskish Mountains on my way to Cahermore. Mid-afternoon I rounded the end of the Beara Peninsula where it was a little more level going for which I was so grateful. Out to sea there were numerous small islands which had some very high mountains with sharp peaks. On the road going towards Eyeries I didn't see one person. It was so quiet up on those mountains with the only sound being that of sheep and lambs bleating as dusk was approaching. Around teatime I came to the top of a very steep hill and was so relieved to see a village in the valley below and close to the sea. It was a Allihies. With the aid of my directory, given to me at the campsite in Durrus, I located the Coulagh Bay House B&B run by Jason and Denise Fegan. During the conversation we had when I arrived I discovered that Denise's sister, who was at the moment there in Allihies on holiday, lives about 100 yards from my sister Kathleen in Rostrevor.

Once again I set about the contents of my panniers to see what I could do to lighten my load even more. I dumped quite a lot of clothes which I wasn't going to need now that the weather was so much warmer and especially if I was going to be staying in hostels and B&Bs. I even binned the thick imitation leather cover on my address book and put the sheets in a small plastic bag. I also went to the extent of cutting all the pages from my travel guides which didn't relate to Ireland's coastal areas. Next to go in the bin was that half of the tarpaulin I carried to cover my cycle at night. I then altered the other half of it, which I used to completely cover my tent right down to the ground, by reducing its size so that its ends would fasten to my tent cords. This would almost give me the equivalent of a two skin tent and would to some extent reduce the condensation on the tent. Pleased with my effort I settled down for the night.

Amongst the other guests at breakfast I met a couple called Linda and Chris Harrington from Wetherby in North Yorkshire. We exchanged details so that we could get in touch when I eventually returned home. What a small world we live in? At an adjacent breakfast table I was amazed to see a rather large American man calmly take out a syringe from a small case and quite openly injected himself in his upper arm. He made no attempt to hide what he was doing and didn't even break off from his conversation he was having with his wife opposite. I assumed he was giving himself a routine insulin injection but nevertheless I could well imagine the effect that sight would have had on some people I know who would have either fainted, or been sick or both!

I set off immediately after breakfast, in brilliant sunshine and a really strong breeze in off the sea which would greatly help me up the steep hills I knew were waiting up ahead on the road to Kenmare. I had been going less than an hour and was labouring up a particularly steep hill when a car, with four women, stopped to enquire if I was doing this cycling for a charity. Apparently they had seen me at three different location back along the coast within the past week and wanted to contribute to whatever charity I was involved with. We had a chat for about fifteen minutes then they drove on but when I reached the top of the hill they had stopped and had a drink ready for me plus some sweet cake. I was ready for it. Altogether that day a total of four cars, each with American tourists, stopped to ask the same sort of questions.

Mid-afternoon I was approaching the village of Ardgroom when I saw at the roadside a sign stating 'TEAS, COFFEES, HOME BAKING'. A bit of home baking I really fancied so I stopped at the house called, 'Kathleen's Cottage'. I was taken to the kitchen table by the said Kathleen and within minutes I was having tea with fresh, hot, home-made bread which she had just baked. I hadn't tasted delicious home-made bread like that for years. A local man called Barry McCreadie was there. He told me that the famous Irish singer Ruby Murray was his aunt.

As darkness fell that evening I was into County Kerry and had already set up the tent on the Creeven Lodge

Caravan Park, by the Healey Pass Road, in Lauragh Village. It had been a long hard slog all day and I was ready for a good nights rest. This site was not only for caravans but also campers. It had a very clean kitchen in which tea, milk, sugar and lots of biscuits were supplied. The showers and the tea etc. were all included in the very reasonable price. The only problem I had was with the hordes of very hungry midges which were everywhere but thanks to the insect repellent and the improvised head nets idea from 'The Black Cat' shop almost a week ago now I was immune to their attacks.

The following day, Saturday, 30th May I had been cycling for one month. It saw me well on my way towards Kenmare in wonderful sunshine and not a breeze of any sort which made cycling very hot going. Down to my left was the wide Kenmare River. I looked more like a lough. On the other side of the river was the notorious Ring of Kerry which everyone said would be my greatest challenge to my fitness. They were the highest mountains I had seen so far. At least from this morning's weather forecast I could expect a sunny day for my tussle with the Ring of Kerry. On this stretch of the road I became acutely aware of an accident risk which I hadn't experienced to date, particularly on sharp bends on the downhill stretches. The problem was an almost 3ft wide band of loose gravel along the roadside. As the road was narrow all vehicles, except when meeting other vehicles, would naturally drive in the centre of the road hence the abnormal accumulation of loose gravel at either side. One incident in which I skidded on this gravel on a downhill bend, but luckily didn't fall off my bike, brought the risk sharply into focus. On some of the bends where I could see any approaching traffic I could ride in the middle part of the road where it was safe to do so but not on bends where I couldn't see ahead. I was surprised that this danger hadn't been highlighted by warning road signs.

In Kenmare I got stocked up on food in preparation for the journey around the Ring of Kerry and the rest of the Iveragh Peninsula. A road sign at Kenmare showed me that it was 77km to Caharsiveen which was just to the north of the most westerly point of the peninsula. I took the road which, apart from one section of about 10 miles where it looped away inland, followed the coast almost to the end of the peninsula. By midday I was in the town of Sneem which was very busy with locals and tourists.

On the outskirts to Sneem I came to a house by the roadside which had larger than life size portraits painted on all the outside walls of the house. They were of famous Irish playwrights, poets and historic figures. I stopped to admire them and saw the artist working on his latest wall painting. He was copying a Picasso. As an amateur artist myself I couldn't resist having a chat with him. I was taken into the house where I met his wife Bernadette. Over coffee, cakes and bars of lovely chocolate he told me all about his passion for art and showed me several large canvasses of his work. His name was Bartholomew Fitzpatrick. This was their summer holiday home but his other home is in Dublin. As a sort of reward for my refreshments, I completed painting a large section of wall where he was going to do his next painting and then I got on my way.

Next stop was the Sea Crest Hostel. After booking in I took my food to the kitchen and enjoyed the new found feeling of home-from-home as I got the cooker going. There were several other travellers there, all couples. They were from Norway, Holland, Denmark and from Dublin. I was the only male! I had a large 4 bed room to myself. Next morning it was through Caherdaniel and past Lake Currane on my right where there were already several rod fishermen in action. In Waterville, a nice tidy smart looking seaside town I joined some people having their photographs taken by a statue of Charlie Chaplain. A plaque nearby stated he often came here on holiday and to visit friends in the area. Shortly after that I turned down a narrow coast road towards the town of Ballinskelligs but it brought me back up to the same road a few miles further on but I was rewarded with a panoramic view of several islands, some large, some small, some close to the coast but some quite far out at sea. Near Caherciveen I had a great view down over Valencia Island and the harbour. There were boats everywhere both out at sea and around the harbour. Most of them seemed to be fishing boats.

All along this stretch of road where I had just come there were numerous waterfalls. The waterfalls were so high that their sound dominated all other sounds. For miles and miles it was one continuous sound which dominated all other sounds of the countryside. The

water was obviously coming from high up on the Slieve
Misk Mountains. It struck me that here was a valuable
source of power which could be used to operate
electricity turbines for domestic use. On the highest
point of the mountain overlooking Valencia Island there
was a much neglected statue of the Virgin Mary looking
out to sea. The kneeling stone, which should have been
in front of the statue, was laid some yards away upside
down. On an impulse I replaced it and put several
smaller stones around two sides of it to tidy it up a bit.
Its untidiness was in sharp contrast to that of other
similar statues and grottos I had seen so far. Perhaps that
was due to its remote location.

This was the hottest day I had experienced so far. I
decided to stop and get into some cooler clothes. Along
the road I abandoned my 'Noddy' blanket. I hung it on a
gate with a note stating where I had found it. Next I cut
off the legs of my lightweight trousers I had bought the
previous week to make them into shorts and instead of
my baseball cap I got out my 'Tilley' hat to wear. My
waterproofs I fastened to my rear carrier and put on my
fluorescent sleeveless jacket. The space created by the
disposal of the 'Noddy' blanket made room in one of the
panniers for the grey lightweight jacket with 18 pockets
for storing cash and personal belongings which I had
worn daily from the beginning. Now I felt I was dressed
for the good weather that was surely bound to be from
now on. I had no sooner set off cycling again when I
saw a large piece of clear plastic on a wide grass verge
by the side of the road. When I inspected it I saw that it
was clean, strong and would be an excellent substitute

for my much heavier piece of tarpaulin I was using to put over my tent. So, I cut it to the size of the tarpaulin then rolled up the tarpaulin and tied it to a nearby farm gateway. The plastic was so much lighter and took up less room on my bike.

As I got to Kilorglin the wind changed to blowing from inland but it was still only a light breeze which helped to keep me cool. In Milltown there was a national bodrun championship taking place. The town was so packed with people I had to turn away from the pedestrian blocked main street and make my way through back streets to the other side of town. A big marquee just off the main street was where the competition was being held hence the problem. However, I learnt from a few people stood by the town's main bridge, that a big fight had developed in the main street between some gipsies and people who had come for the competition and that had added to the congestion. As we talked two police cars rushed past towards the crowded main street. The next thing was a group of about 10 to 15 young men, in various stages of undress, came running from the direction of the main street followed by a policeman. I could hear the very lively bodrun music over loudspeakers but decided it was time to move off.

The next town on my schedule was to be Inch where I had been told there was a very nice campsite close to the sea. I felt I could just make it before darkness came if I put some more weight on the pedals! I found the campsite without any problem. It was called 'SAMMY'S

CAFE, RESTAURANT". The cafe and restaurant were beside the beach with the camping area on the opposite side of the approach road. I got set up in the field which was almost full of other campers, caravans and motorhomes. This was the busiest campsite I had yet been on yet it was by far the cheapest at only 2 Euros for the night.

I got chatting to a most helpful couple from Dublin, Maira and Michael Myers, who were parked close to me in their motorhome. He had been in the Irish Army a number of years, was also trained as a triathlete. From his combined SAS type training and his knowledge of cycling he gave me expert advice on not only what I needed to carry but how to travel light whether on foot or on a bike. Together we spread out every single item I was carrying on my large plastic sheet. He went through it in a few minutes. The result was that I discarded almost two panniers full of everything from clothing to footwear and bedding. In place of a bag of cycle tools he gave me an extremely lightweight and compact set which fitted every nut, bolt and screw on my bike. In adjusting the height of my saddle and handlebars he demonstrated the capabilities of small tool set he gave me. He also gave me a new special sweat proof top to wear when cycling. It doesn't hold the sweat. I wished I had met him before I started out on this venture. I promised to return the tool kit to him when I eventually got back to England.

By mid-morning I set off, so much lighter, on my way to

Dingle. I was helped along once again by a wind from behind which compensated for the hills on the way. Several pleasure boats were out in the bay including many with sails of varying sizes and colours but there didn't seem to be any sort of competition in progress as the boats were all going to and fro. A few miles from Dingle I saw a sign to the 'South Pole Inn' and decided to investigate the reason for the rather special name. It was opened in the 1920s by a local man in who had been with Scott and later Shakleton on various expeditions to the South Pole in the early 1900s. His history, displayed all over the interior of the pub, makes for very interesting reading about a very brave man. The pub, its car park and roadway were packed with tourists. There I treated myself to lunch.

The midday sun was so hot as I rode along the straight flat road towards Dingle that the tar was actually melting. The roadway ahead shimmered as if it was covered in water. On the outskirts of Dingle a car load of Americans stopped me to enquire what I was doing as they had seen me further back along the coast on three or four occasions during this past week. When I had finished telling them there was the usual round of photographs then off they went. Tourists were everywhere in Dingle but I had a ride around the town while the very kind young woman in the Tourist Office charged up my two mobile phones. I then rode on seeking the coast road and hopefully a nice cool sea breeze. Verity Harbour was crowded with boats of all description and no doubt was the source of all those out in the bay.

As I rounded the end of the peninsula there was a great view of the world famous Blasket Islands silhouetted against the setting sun. A little way further on I booked into Campail Teach An Aragall Campsite, had a meal and an early night.

Midges were everywhere the following day. I had to put my Tilley Hat net on in such a way that the net hung down in front of my face as I went along to prevent midges getting in my eyes, nose and mouth. The net cured the midge problem and was better than the sunglasses as it didn't darken everything. I didn't dare use my newly acquired nylon stocking midge net in case I gave some unsuspecting passer- by a heart attack at the sight!

I kept heading northwards on a very narrow twisty road via Ballydavid which took me back to Dingle. A short way outside Dingle I met up with Jerry Cooke, a young man cycling from Dublin on a circuit of the south coast. He explained to me why my milometer didn't work. It was, he said, due to the luggage on the front carrier blocking the signal from the sensor on the front wheel getting to the milometer on the handlebars. He said that the most reliable milometer was the type which had a cable connecting both the sensor and the unit on the handlebars. I removed the things from the front carrier and sure enough when I rode the bike a little way along the road the milometer worked perfectly. Next I got out the instrument's instructions but they contained no such advice. To say I was annoyed with myself at not thinking of that in the first place would be a gross understatement! Well, it was too late to bother about that now so I put the things back on the carrier and got on my way, but I was nevertheless very grateful to Jerry for the information.

For the second time today I headed north, this time on the road which would take me over the notorious Connor Pass. I managed to accomplish it without dismounting but it was one hard slog, even in bottom gear. This route was all mountains with the odd habitation and small farms along the way. Wild birds and animals such as rabbits, hares, squirrels and even foxes were everywhere. In a few places I saw rats in the roadway eating the carcases of rabbits which had obviously been killed by vehicles. From the northern coast road the views over both Brandon Bay and Tralee bay were a treat. I didn't see any people until a short distance from Strabally where there were a lot of the usual farming activities going on in the fields. In some instances horses and tractors were working in the same field which was an unusual sight. Sheep grazing at the roadside didn't even bother to look up as I rode past quite close to them. An unusual sight, in that environment anyway, was a Collie sheepdog with a litter of three very young pups. It was near the road so I called to it but instead of coming towards me where I could take a photograph, it slunk off followed by its pups. It was near to dusk when I arrived at Woodlands Caravan and Camping Park on Dingle Road, Tralee. This was the most modern campsite I had yet visited. It had water, electricity and lighting on every pitch plus a car parking space. The pitches were all level and large enough to take very big tents or caravans or motorhomes. Toilets and all the other facilities were immaculate.

I set off early to make the most of the morning before the sun got around to overheating everything and me in particular. All went well until a short way past Fenit when large farm machinery of every description started to meet and overtake me on that very narrow twisty road. Everything was ok until I got too close to the long briars which overhung the road at infrequent intervals from thorn hedges which were also full of large nettles. Of course it had to be my first day of riding in shorts and short sleeve top. Well, one very long briar blocked my path just as one of these big machines was about to overtake me. I hadn't time to stop and certainly couldn't swerve out to miss it. I braked but too late. The briar had ripped the skin of my left leg. Before I knew what was happening I overbalanced and fell into the hedge on top of briars and nettles. I lay there until the last in a queue of four machines went past. The young man in the last one did stop and ask if I was ok but I put a brave face on things and said, "Yeah I'm OK. Don't worry" then off he went. When I got up my arms and legs was suffering from nettle stings, assorted cuts and scratches from the thorns but fortunately nothing more serious. The back wheel of the bike, which projected somewhat into the path of the machines, narrowly escaped being squashed. Altogether I felt I had been very lucky as I could have fallen under the machine which was passing me at the time. I could see where the hedges on both sides of the road had obviously never been trimmed. The only attention they got was from vehicles which brushed passed close to them and that kept them from becoming totally overgrown. I found a nearby gateway where I sought refuge from more passing farm vehicles and did my best to apply First Aid. In the field I saw lots of dockens and used their juice to quell the nettle stings. Next thing I did was change out of my shorts and short sleeve top. In future I would ensure that I was having my breakfast between 8am and 9 am to lessen the risk of falling foul of farm traffic like today.

A few miles further on I saw some writing on the road which really puzzled me. It was the words 'LOWER BODY' in 6 inch high capital letters written in yellow paint and underlined in yellow. The writing which was quite neat was about two inches thick as was the underlining. Its total width on the road was about three feet and was only on the left hand carriageway when facing north. It had only recently been applied to the road surface. The first instance of this I saw didn't concern me too much but helped take my mind off my suffering arms and legs. However, over the next three miles approximately I saw the exact same sign on the road four times. There were no such signs on the other side of the road. I made enquiries from various people along the way, including the supervisor of a team of road workers, with success. In Ballyheige I took the coast road around Kerry Head peninsula via Dreenagh. Some of the cycling enthusiasts I had met along the way here had mentioned the very popular annual triathlon which is held here every year. It was all very quiet as I passed through. I followed the same road along to Ballyduff, over the Cashen Bridge and on to Ballybunion. Records which state that this area has the highest and the most mountains in Ireland were not far wrong. On this road so far I felt I had cycled up the sides of most of them. I couldn't get to my pre-booked hostel at Tabret soon enough! Along this stretch of road I passed two small cemeteries with quite elaborate tombs above ground level. I also saw two fields, in different areas, where there were ordinary stones laid out in the form of a graveyard without any markings whatsoever on the stones. I took them to be from the Famine times. At the second one a car was parked at the gateway. Its occupants were taking photographs of the stones but there were no signs anywhere I could see that stated either was a graveyard.

On a grassy verge some two miles on the Tabret side of Ballylongford I stopped where I saw a pair of men's socks, white, brand new, with the price label still on them. They were clean and dry. I put them in my panniers and carried on. They would no doubt soon come in useful.

In Tarbert I booked into the 'Ferry House Holiday Hostel' hostel run by Ted and Margaret O'Connell. They said I could put my bike 'out the back' where it would be in a shed under lock and key instead of simply leaving it in the yard at the front of the hostel. To do this it meant taking the bike through their private part of the hostel. It was very kind of them to let me do this. Also, they said that unless they had a big rush of guests I would be able to have a five bed room to myself. Tabret seemed quite a busy town so I decided to go and have a look around the shops and have a meal. On the way back to the hostel I came very near to suffering much more bodily harm than when I had fallen into the roadside hedge. A large mongrel dog, restrained only by its lead hooked to the top of a low wooden fence near to a newsagents' shop, did its mighty best to eat me alive! As I was walking past it, fortunately some four feet away, it suddenly lunged at me with teeth bared all ready for action. It really went berserk, rearing up on its hind legs and barking furiously. I lengthened my stride somewhat until I was at a safe distance but it was still going mad. Its owner never appeared to investigate. At the hostel shortly afterwards I was looking out my bedroom window when I saw the same dog. It was trotting along sedately at the side of a very attractive young woman. I wondered if I bore some resemblance to her abusive boyfriend / husband or was it something about my appearance? I dreaded to think of what might have happened to me if I had cycled past that dog somewhere when it wasn't on a lead. With that thought in mind I got out my "Dog Repellent Spray" and promised myself that I would have it very close at hand in future. One such scare was enough for anyone!

The Tabret / Killmer ferry trip the following morning took only about half an hour. After that it was only a short ride to Kilrush where I found that the weekly Farmers' Market was already well under way. There was every variety a farm animals there plus equipment of all sorts. Of course there were stalls selling the usual wide range of goods one would see in any market town. The main street was far too busy for cycling so I got off my bike and walked. I caught up on an elderly lady going in the same direction and asked her she could recommend a good place for a breakfast. "It's The Quayside you need" she said. "Come on I'll show you". She asked what I was doing and I told her. She not only showed me where it was but while I made my bike secure she went inside and told the owners, James and Margaret Tubridy, about me. She turned down my offer of a cup of tea and was off into the crowd. I had a tea, made with real tea leaves, and a very big breakfast, at a table on the footpath. It was great to sit and watch the bustling market activity whilst I was enjoying breakfast. Right in front of me a man had stall and beside it on the tarmac he had a stack of all sorts of things spread out. On old man, perhaps in his sixties, came to stand by the items on the tarmac. He was wearing an old dark suit and a wide brimmed old white hat. He had a half open bag in one hand and a walking stick in the other. I had seen him at the next stall a few moments before and noticed that he kept picking up various items and putting them down again without even looking at them. He came to the stall in front of me and was using his stick to move some of the things around that were in the pile. Then, when the stall holder was busy serving two women this man pulled a new looking flat cap from the side of the pile with his walking stick and slid it around the back of the stall out of sight of the stallholder where he quickly picked it up on the end of his stick and put it into the plastic bag. He then went back to poking around in the pile with his stick, spoke a few words to the stallholder and went off to the next stall. I was sure that people sitting in the cafe window area would also have seen what he did. What a cheek he had? I could hardly resist going to the stall holder and telling him what I had seen but then thought better of it. I tried to put it out of my mind but it kept niggling me.

I paid my bill and took a ride down to the quay and then back to get on with my journey. However, there at the top of the street, I saw the man in question waiting to cross the street. Here was my chance. "I saw you steal that cap that's in your bag", I told him. "I know you and if you don't put it back in the next ten minutes I am going down to tell the man what you did. OK!" He stepped back and stood staring at me wide eyed. "Ten minutes, that's all I'll give you" I repeated and at that I rode off. I deliberately turned down another street a few yards away as if I was going back towards the stall area but of course I didn't. I made my way around a few other street and came back onto the main road out of town towards Kilkee. I felt a bit more at ease with my conscience now but realised that I had in many ways put my personal safety at risk whilst in that area. I doubted if he would have taken my advice but at least it might have given him something to worry about.

A short way after Moyasta on the road to Kilkee I turned southwards to see Ireland's 'Secret Peninsula' as the Loop Head Peninsula is often described. It is supposed to be the most desolate place in the whole country where all you hear is the screech of seagulls and the crash of waves on the rock pillars which jut out into the sea. I rode down via Doonaha then on to Kilbaha right on the end of the tip of the peninsula. Sure enough it lived up to its nick name. There were a few cars there and several different groups of people having picnics. I stayed long enough to feel the peace and quiet of the place, apart from the calling of the seagulls and sure enough, the crashing of the waves.

In a village called Kilferagh a man with a lawnmower was cutting grass on the verge outside his house. I stopped for a chat and a rest. He was called Ted and as soon as I stopped he said, "You are just in time for a mug of coffee. Do you like coffee" and as he spoke a little girl came out to him from the house with his mug of coffee. He sent her back in for another one but this time his wife came out with it. "Have we got any holy water left Mary"? And off back in went Mary to return with a half bottle full of 'holy water' – the fairly common name for Poitín which can only be loosely described as home brew whisky. I didn't see how much he put in my coffee but I was sure it would be a lot for when he had put some in his coffee the bottle was nearly empty. He was called Jerry and the little girl, probably his grand daughter, was called Theresa. We all sat on the low garden wall and I had them to tell me about life on the peninsula while we drank the coffee and finished off a big, newly baked rhubarb and apple pie which Mary brought out for us all. Ted was all for putting the remainder of the Poitín in my coffee if he got a chance but I wouldn't let him. I was worried that I might not be able to ride the bike safely on the amount I already had in my coffee. An hour or so later, with my head spinning from the effect of the ' holy water', I was back on my bike. Ted's parting words were, "That little nip will strengthen your legs and lower the hills for you this evening". In my mirror I could see him pouring the remainder of the bottle into his mug. I enjoyed my visit to this 'desolate place' a lot more than I expected.

In Kilkee I came to a 'Quayside Cafe' which I took to be a branch of the one in Kilrush. The two young Polish girls in charge didn't know anything about the Kilrush Cafe but that didn't matter. The Poitín was definitely having an effect on me and I was ready for a quick break. I finished up having two teapots of tea and some sort of pie which neither they nor I could figure out what it was but it tasted good.

North of Kilkee I was coasting down a long hill when I noticed a man standing on my side of the road. As I got closer I saw that he was leaning on some long handled thing like a rake or fork and was watching me approaching. I saw hedge clippings near the wall behind him and assumed he was cutting the hedge. When I got to within a few hundred yards of him I got a strong impulse to stop and help him. In my later years I have come to recognise such impulses as some form of psychic message and wherever possible I act on them, often with unbelievable results. This was to be one of those instances. I stopped by him. He was a well-built man of about 60 years and obviously was making a start on cutting the hedge. Without giving a thought as to what to say I came out with, "I understand you need someone to help you". In a way I felt so stupid at saying that and for a moment thought that the Poitín really was getting to me. The man took a step back and, with a smile on his face gave me a long look for a second or two then said, "Can you take off that hat till I see who you are?" I took it off, now not knowing what to say. He then said, "Are you a Garda". Well that gave me an opening. I told him I wasn't but I was a retired Police Inspector from England and told him my name and very briefly said what I was doing. I finished by telling him about the feeling that came over me as I came towards him and explained that was why I said what I did. "Put that bike down and come in the house while I tell you something you are not going to believe" he said. I did as he asked. He poured us both a mug of tea then related to me the following events. The previous night he had accidentally fallen in the bathroom and injured his right shoulder. His daughter, who was in the next room, had asked if he was ok and he said he was. His shoulder really hurt after that but being a macho type of man he didn't complain to his wife about his shoulder last night. However, after his wife and daughter had gone out for the day on urgent family business, he checked his shoulder and thought he had possibly dislocated his right collar bone. He then decided he would wait until tomorrow when they were due to be out again all day and he would then seek medical help before saying anything to either of them. A short while before I came on the scene he had attempted to cut the hedge but found his shoulder was too painful to continue and was deliberating what to do when I stopped. He said he at first thought I was someone from the Gardaí that knew him and just was offering to help him.

I examined him, using my knowledge of First Aid, and saw that his collar bone was indeed dislocated. It needed attention and I told him so. He wouldn't hear of it. He was adamant that it would wait until the next day. I knew there and then what to do. I brought my bike in off the road, changed out of my cycling outfit and went outside where I set about cutting the top and sides of the rather high, unruly hedge. Jerry came and helped a little with sweeping with one hand and making tea. It took about three hours to finish it and put the clippings on the waste land across the road and tidy up. Now an even more unbelievable coincidence revealed itself. In 1961 a Garda officer named Mike Reid was a colleague of Jerry's in Dublin. Mike was then the Irish Amateur Boxing Association Champion. He and I boxed each other in the International Police Boxing Championship finals in The Albert Hall in London in 1961. He beat me and went on to become that year's champion once again. At this point Jerry said that I just had to stop the night with him and the family. As it was now after teatime I said that I would so long as I could pay for my accommodation but he wouldn't hear any talk about payment. Above all else he didn't want his wife and daughter to know about his injury. He said that he would simply explain that as we both had the same work background and especially as I had helped him with the hedge he had insisted that I stay the night. He said that in any case up until last year their house was in fact a B&B so my stay wouldn't be a problem. He made me promise not to tell either his wife or daughter about his injury.

When Jerry's wife Mary and their daughter Aine came home he explained as we had agreed. I felt rather unhappy about that idea as it made me seem like someone who was looking for a night's bed on the cheap and had helped with the hedge for that reason but we all had tea together then sat talking until quite late. Shortly before bedtime, Jerry and Mary were out of the room and I took that opportunity to tell Aine about her father's injury and about my promise to him not to tell. We agreed that in the morning, after I had gone, she would ask her father about his shoulder and make sure that he got immediate treatment. As soon as we all had breakfast the next morning I got going. As I rode northwards again I had plenty to occupy my mind after such an almost unbelievable series of coincidences.

On the outskirts of Spanish Point, where I stopped for a short break and the usual cup of tea at a small cafe I had a great conversation with the proprietors, Gerard and Marie O'Leary who treated me to a little bit of the history of the area. Apparently it was named after the Spanish Armada which lost so many of its ships along this coast in 1588. Visitors were everywhere in the town when I arrived. On the beach the high waves were being enjoyed by numerous surfers. I found it quite relaxing to sit and watch them for a while then had a short stroll along the beach enjoying an ice cream. Within an hour I moved on towards my next gaol, namely the Cliffs of Moher which held a special place in my memory.

Quite quickly, thanks to a nice back wind which helped me up the hills. I got there much sooner than I expected. I stopped in the gateway to the water treatment plant at the top of the cliffs where ten years before while I was travelling in a van in that area on holiday I had parked up overnight. I was at first taken to be a gipsy by a nearby farmer and no doubt by other passing locals. I befriended the farmer when he stopped to enquire why I was there. A drystone wall at one side of the gateway was in a bad state of repair due, the farmer told me, by inconsiderate visitors climbing over it to have a view of the cliffs rather than using the nearby footpath provided for that purpose. After he had left I decided that I would rebuild the wall for him as a token of my appreciation for how nice he had been to me. Using my rather limited previous experience of building such walls I immediately began rebuilding it. Besides I felt that passers-by would now think I was a builder hard at work rather than a gipsy setting up camp in the gateway. I thoroughly enjoyed the self-imposed task and by nightfall it was complete. The following morning the farmer was surprised at my efforts. He offered to give me a job immediately repairing similar walls on his farm. He said that it was hard to find anyone who wanted to do dry stone wall building it as it was such a slow, time consuming job. He offered to pay me for the work I had done but of course I wouldn't hear of it. I told him I had thoroughly enjoyed doing it and that in any case the exercise would have done me some good. "You must be a glutton for punishment" he said. "If I had biked it all the way around the country to here, the last thing I would think about doing would be to start building a wall for exercise. Don't leave 'till I get back". Off he went in his van and came back shortly afterwards with some fresh home-made bread, butter and two dozen eggs and had me to promise him that next time I was the area I was to call on him and stay at his farm instead of in the gateway.

On this visit I found that the walls on both sides of the gate, plus the gate itself had been replaced. A high metal fence now surrounded the water treatment plant. The new walls had been built with stone reinforced by concrete and the gateway had been narrowed by large stones and soil, no doubt to deter anyone from parking there. I did think of paying a visit to the farmer but felt sure that if I did I wouldn't get away until tomorrow. It was too early to think about stopping for the night. Using the footpath I went and had a look at the wonderful panoramic view out over the Atlantic. Seagulls were gliding to and fro far below. Some other type of sea birds were constantly diving from a great height into the water, disappearing for a minute or more then resurfacing with a fish they had caught. When they had caught a fish they flew back to perch on the cliff face, no doubt to feed their young ones. It was so peaceful up on there on the cliff tops that I treated myself to a siesta. I lay down on the grass and fell asleep only to be awakened about half an hour later by a Cocker Spaniel dog which had come to have a sniff at my face. Had I been snoring again I wondered? Its owners, a couple walking nearby, apologised to me, called the dog and were about to put it on a lead but I said they were not to worry as it was time I was on the move.

My next stop just had to be Lisdoonvarna. On the way there on the main road a car drew level with me at one stage. They were a couple I had met back in Tralee. He was Irish and she was Lithuanian and they were on their way back home to Dundalk. They said they had been hoping they would see me again on their way home and had actually taken the longer route via the coastal roads to see how I was progressing. They wanted to have some photographs taken with me they said and also get my details so that they could eventually buy my book about my experiences on the trip. The lady passed me a large bag of sweets plus a few bars of chocolates as they drove off, tooting the car horn and waving to me, before I thought of getting their names.

A little way further on I had one of those 'once in a lifetime' experiences where I saw a sign over a garage with a unique feature in its title. It read 'Pat Foudy And Daughter'. That was the first time I had ever seen the title 'Daughter' included in a business name. Always it was either 'Son' or 'Sons'.

Lisdoonvarna wasn't on my coastal route but no way could I bypass that town without visiting it. It is world famous for its annual September festival when men and women go there in the hope of meeting up with a suitable lifetime partner. The centre of attraction in the town is the 'Matchmaker Bar'. It is one of the main places in the town where some local men, dubbed as 'Matchmakers' set about the task of matching up suitable couples. When I got into Lisdoonvarna it was very busy indeed but for some reason the 'Matchmaker Bar' was closed. I photographed it featuring its now well-known slogan: "Marriages Are Made in Heaven but Most People Meet in the Matchmaker Bar" emblazoned across its front wall. Four middle aged men were leaning on the wall and noticed me stop. I doubted if they could be 'matchmakers' looking for work! One of them said, "He'll be open soon". Jokingly I asked them if they were waiting to go in and see about finding a wife. One said, "No way. I have one at home that I would gladly sell or trade in for a new model. Why, is that what you are after? I said I wouldn't mind finding one but if I did I would have to put a deposit on her and come back for her with a car as there was no more room left on my bike. One of them said, "I can tell you something for nothing. No woman will want to know you when you're dressed like that but anyway it's not matchmaking time 'till September". And so the banter went on between us until I was ready to move on. They had got to know all about me and what I was doing so I asked if I could have their first names. They were Terry, John, and Jimmy but the fourth man, who had earlier commented about his wife said, "You're not having my name. She'd have my guts for garters will that one, if she ever found out what I'd said". I took a short ride around the town. In one place I saw a life size stone carving of a couple dancing. Almost every shop had some sort of memorabilia to do with the match making industry which had made the town famous worldwide. Perhaps I might come back one September and try my luck.

In the meantime it was back westwards to the R477 and up around the coast with the Aran Islands lying far away out of the mouth of Galway Bay. Altogether I saw three passenger boats out in the bay, two of which appeared to be on their way to the islands and one coming away from them. Again, like further back along the way here, I promised myself that another time I would come back and visit all of these off shore islands. Like the Blasket Islands they too are famous the world over as are the numerous books written about them and their inhabitants. The scenery along that road up to Black Head was breathtakingly beautiful with a hint of ancient landscape all around, wild waves lashing the rocky beaches. Cottages were everywhere with a good mixture of those used exclusively in the summer season and those occupied by the local people. At one point the road had been quarried out of the mountainside and everywhere there were dry stone walls, built many years ago and still standing in perfection. A very old style lighthouse stood out by the waves surrounded by an unusual bed of rock which looked as if it had been chopped into equal size sections all lined up in rows. Some distance away I saw a house literally perched on the cliff edge. Everything I saw about Black Head made me feel that it was truly a place as unusual as its name.

After Black Head it was on to Ballyvaughan, then

Belaclugga. Signposts showed the next big town to be
Burren but after the hard slog from Black Head in a
strong side wind in from the sea, an overcast sky and
dusk fast approaching I felt it was time to seek out
somewhere to stay. As well as my tiredness I was having
trouble with my left shoulder which was still aching
badly after my very recent fall into the roadside hedge. I
stopped to help two women who were trying to get two
stubborn cows off the road and into a field. I asked if
they knew of any B&Bs where I could stay. "Down
there on your left there is a sign for one. The house is
about five minutes up that road" so off I went and sure
enough there was a sign 'CIL B&B'. I was so pleased I
had asked the women because the sign was almost
totally obscured by bushes and weeds. The five minutes
slipped into forty five minutes so I waved down a man
approaching on a bicycle. He wasn't so sure if there was
one he said but I should ask at the farmhouse at the top
of the hill. That I did and found that my luck was in. The
farmer, called Tommy Fahy, said the B&B belonged to
his family. "It's just back down there on your left" he
said, "We have just had it all done up so you'll see a lot
of rubble out front. Someone will be there". I had seen
the house as I passed but there were no lights on in it
and there certainly wasn't a B&B sign anywhere near it.
As I pulled up a car drove in behind me and Donnacha
Fahy, the son, introduced himself. He explained that his
mother, Theresa, was visiting family in Australia and he
was looking after the house which was indeed a B&B
and apologised for the sign which was lying in the grass
by the gate. "All this rubble will be gone tomorrow" he
said "and the sign will be back up. Sorry about that". I
was pleased that the sign hadn't been up. If the sign had

been up, I think the fact that it was in darkness plus all the rubble I would have given up and camped in one of the nearby fields.

What a surprise I got when Donnacha took me inside. It was a six bedroom house where everything was brand new. He showed me round and said I could sleep in any of the rooms I wished. All the beds were made up and ready for guests. Apparently guests were arriving on Sunday evening but Donnacha said I could stay that night and the next night if I wished but I would need to be away by Sunday lunchtime which was when the guests were expected. I assured him that I would only be staying overnight and would be gone early in the morning. He showed me how everything worked and said I could help myself to any of the food in the cupboards. He even switched on the big wide screen television and said, "Now you can sit here and relax and look after the place for us". He wouldn't hear of any discussion about the price saying that it would be good that I was there to look after the place. During our conversation I spoke of the problem with my shoulder whereupon he pulled out a kitchen chair, sat me down and gave me quick session of physiotherapy which completely got rid of the ache. Apparently he had some knowledge of physiotherapy and assured me that afterwards my shoulder condition would improve. He didn't realise how grateful I was at the thought that the dull ache in my shoulder might go. What a super young man! Next he handed me the bunch of house keys with the words, "It's all yours now. Sleep well. Put the keys through the door if you do go off early tomorrow" and was gone but as I was bringing in my panniers he returned with a carton of milk and a loaf of bread.

Once again I could hardly believe everything that had happened that day, but especially my luck in finding this place to stay overnight. I made some supper, put my mattress on the big rug in front of the living room fire and watched some television before dropping off into a much needed sleep. I was awake soon after daylight, got a shower, breakfast and was putting my panniers back on the bike when Donnacha called past on his way to work and to check that I was ok. As I left shortly before lunch time I put the keys through the letterbox as he asked plus my estimate of what it would have cost me elsewhere. Later in the day I discovered that I had left behind two of my maps which had lots of details on them relating to places I had stayed plus other details.

Near Kinvarra I stopped for a break at 'The Topas Excel Stop And Shop' where I got into conversation with the owner, Paddy O'Loughlin. I found him a very interesting man to talk to, true student of this life as one might describe him. He told me of an occasion recently when he met Brian Keenan who had been a hostage with Terry Waite in the Middle East. Brian had stopped for diesel for his car but still took time to talk to him about all sorts of things in life. Paddy took a great interest in all the whys and wherefores of my trip. At first he thought I was doing it for some charitable cause and was surprised that I decided to do it simply as a celebration of my 70th birthday and the furtherance of my enjoyment at seeing new places and making new acquaintances. He liked that idea. While I was there I wrote a note to Donnacha, plus a stamped, self-addressed envelope, asking him to please send the maps on to me and posted it nearby.

On my way to Kilcolgan the views over Galway Bay now included Spiddle and Barna and Salthill, all of which I hope to visit before that day was over. By early afternoon I was in Galway and made my way to the Square as did hundreds of other tourist types. My thoughts on entering the town were of my late mother who so often spoke of her trips into Galway with her parents. Many times she mentioned the Square where I was now. One thing for sure was that she never witnessed what I saw there that day. On top of a three foot high, approximately four inches diameter wooden post by a memorial in the centre of the Square there was a youth dressed as a clown. He was in full make up complete with bowler hat and white gloves. At the base of the post was a tin bowl into which onlookers could throw money. When they did he would go into action. He would make a deep bow with quick jerky actions as if he was a robot. He would then, with the same movements, return to the erect position. Throughout he stared straight ahead without any expression whatsoever on his face. People continually posed beside him for photographs; some tried to get him to laugh or smile but it was all in vain. Little children went over and touched his feet. Probably some of them didn't think he was a real person. I finished my ice cream, put some money in the tin bowl, got a deep bow and then I was on my way satisfied that I had seen a really talented street performer in action.

I rode out to my mother's home village of Corcullen and visited her parent's grave. I rode past her homeplace then took the road to Barna with a heavy heart. Had I called on any of my many relatives in the area I would still have been there a week later! On the northern side of Galway bay I had a view of the mountainous coastline where I had been earlier. The evening sun lit up Slieve Elna and the other lesser peaks of the Burren. Eddy Island and Tawin Island stood out in clear relief. With my binoculars I was certain I could even make out Dungaire Castle. Another day to remember was drawing to a close as I set up camp for the night at Ballyloughane Campsite on the Barna Road. Earlier that afternoon, after I left Corcullen, I made another 'find' by the roadside. This time another a pair of gents' white socks which still had the shop label attached. They had been there a few days as they were wet so I washed them at the campsite and hung them to dry. The next day the ride along the coast to the little town of Rossaveel gave me a view out over the calm waters of Galway Bay and then Cashla Bay with the Aran Islands lying clear in the morning sun. The next part of the road up to Screeb showed me more islands out in Kilkieran Bay than I could count. At Screeb the R340 via Derryrush took me on another even more beautiful set of views out over the same bay and its islands. To my mind this was a perfect example of the pleasure of cycling. There were the now familiar steep hills to overcome but the perfect sunshine and no winds to worry about made it a pure heavenly experience. At Ardmore point I came upon a herd of about twenty donkeys in charge of a young lad and a dog all coming from the opposite direction. I stopped until they got past. I had never seen so many donkeys in one place in my life. I attempted to have a conversation with the boy who was about 12 years of age but he seemed too shy to talk to me. The most I got was that his name was Shaun. I asked him if there was any chance that I could swap my bike for one of his donkeys. His very serious reply was, "I can't. They are my Granddads. You can ask him if you like". I asked him where his granddad was but he ignored me. His attention was more with the care of the donkeys and his concern over a small truck behind me which was also waiting on the herd donkeys to pass. A little bit further along I turned off down a very narrow road which eventually wound its way past what looked like a golf course and then a lake where a lone fisherman on the bank, with his tent, was packing up. That road brought me back onto the main road again at Glinsk. There I sat on a grass bank in the sun and gorged myself on a lot of goodies I had accumulated along the way, including the chocolate I had been given a few days ago by the couple on their way home to Dundalk.

A few miles further on I went off around Bertraghboy Bay and then Ballyconneely Bay past signs to Slyne Head and another golf course. Connemara's National Park was on my right with Bencorr high on the skyline, its peak shrouded in a cloud. Bays and peninsulas by the score were off to my left. This was Connemara at its prettiest. All the way the holiday cottages were in

evidence everywhere but remarkably little sign of
tourists on the road.

I was planning to get close to Westport that night but I
had clearly misjudged the distance involved. Close to
Clifden I booked into the Letterbay Hostel. I was told
that it was almost full to capacity with only my room
left. It sure was crowded. Most were young men and
women. The kitchen was a site of activity to behold but
it was all laughter and shouting with the smell of food
that was almost a meal in itself. I had made only a small
light meal and was happy with that but I was adopted by
a group of young men and women at the next table who
were falling about laughing at all the food they had
unwittingly cooked. They persuaded me to share some
with them. Next thing I had a massive plate of curry
presented to me complete with naan breads and a can of
beer! They were all travelling in cars and were horrified,
especially the women, at the thought of someone of my
age even thinking of cycling all the way around Ireland.
They were great fun and by the time I had finished off
the meal and drank the beer they had all gone to a pub
down the road somewhere. I didn't reckon on getting
much sleep that night on their return but I never heard a
sound. At breakfast there was no sign of the group from
last night but their cars were still in the car park. Two
middle aged women joined me in the kitchen. They
were Jane Norman and her friend Mavis Price. One was
a medium and one a healer. Jane was heavily involved
she said, in 'Action For The Blind' in Teignmouth,
Devon. They were world travellers and we had a long
and ever so interesting a conversation about not only

their work but their travelling experiences. It was almost 10.30 am as I left with still no sight or sound of my young friends from last night. Could they still be at the pub I wondered? In a chat with the manager before I left I was surprised to learn that nowadays the majority of guests were those in cars and on motor cycles. Cyclists he said were a rarity. I was the only cyclist that night.

In Clifden I got some more maps and found that it was about forty five miles to Westport but by the time I had deviated all around the coastline it was going to be about sixty five miles at least. The weather forecast was promising but I had learnt on my way that Irish weather could be very unpredictable and more so along this west coast. North of Clifden I did a detour along a side road through Cleggan and back to the main road again at Moyard. A few miles more and I was off again on a similar road this time through Tullycross and Gowlaun. After Gowlaun I had lunch at the side of a Lake Fee overlooked by the towering Mount Garraun. By taking this route I had missed seeing Kylemore Abbey but that would have to wait until another time. Back on the main road again I passed the northern end of the Maamturk Mountains overlooking Killary Harbour. Soon I was through the town of Leenaun and soon after over the border into Mayo where I headed westwards again. Along here it was all mountains and lakes with the biggest one being Lake Doo. All the way up from north of Clifden I passed several peat bogs with droves of men working hard at cutting the turf by hand using the slane. In a few places there were tractors at work with the new method of harvesting the turf by machine. It was such

176

a sentimental a sight for me. My mind went back to my childhood when my brothers and I and my sister would be there on the bog at Spelga in the Mourne Mountains with my father cutting away at the turf from dawn to dusk and fighting the midges off as we did so. Oddly enough I didn't experience any midges on my trip today. When it wasn't bogs along the way it was forests until I finally got to Louisburgh on the shore of Clew Bay. For the first time on that road I had a sea view out over the bay where its white painted lighthouse gleamed in the afternoon sun. It was well into the evening time but I had hoped to perhaps climb Croagh Patrick. By the time I could see it in the distance it was too late to even think about it. It was now time to think about a hostel or campsite for the night. I found a B&B in Liscareney on the south side of Westport called 'Moher House' run by Mrs. Marion O'Malley. I had a great evening meal and shared with me her obvious excitement at the election of her nephew Peter Flynn in the recent Mayo County Council Elections. The following morning she was still as excited about the news of her nephew as she served up a type of very wholesome breakfast that I have now become accustomed to on my way around Ireland. I hadn't checked my weight since I set out on this trip but I felt sure it would have definitely increased. It was quite early next morning when I reached Newport. It was another beautiful cycle trip along a typical west of Ireland coast road with numerous little islands and miniature peninsulas sticking out into the sea which today was quite choppy. For some reason the usual plethora of boats were absent.

In the centre of Newport I saw a mural which almost covered the gable wall of a building. It had been painted quite professionally and depicted the summary execution, by hanging, of two local priests during one of the early rebellions. The peculiar aspect about the mural was that whilst it gave a lot of information on a plaque below the mural this information did not include the names of the priests. I asked two men who were sitting on a window sill across the road if they knew why the priest's names were not on the plaque. Apparently they hadn't realised that fact about the names of the priests but they knew all about the history of the mural being painted by some locals with the help of a group of foreign boys and girls who were attending a local art college some years ago. I couldn't help but wonder why such and obvious detail was not included.

North of Newport outside the village of Tiernaur I had my most unusual roadside 'find' to date. It was the Irish national flag commonly referred to as 'The Tricolour', complete with tie strings, and was lying on top of some weeds. There was no flagpole or post of any sort nearby from where it could have blown or been removed. A man and little boy passing by couldn't help as to where it might have come from but from its clean condition it had most likely only been there from the night before. I decided, rightly or wrongly, to take it. Already I had in mind a certain sister-in-law of mine who would love to have it at Step Dancing displays and competitions, especially when abroad.

From my new map I decided to have a close look at Achill Island without actually going on to it by taking the route which circumnavigates the peninsula and returns near to where I began the trip around the peninsula. It seemed to be all mountains and forests with cottages around the coast. Its three towns of Corraun, Achill and Tonregee were the typical towns of tourist brochure pictures. In a conversation with a shopkeeper in Corraun I referred to the peninsula as if it was not part of Achill Island. He quickly put me right on that score telling me that it was indeed part of Achill Island separated only from the main island by the Michael Davitt Bridge. I didn't feel that I was even remotely qualified to argue the point. I returned to the same point where I entered this 'island' of mountain and forest and headed north again. It had been a tiring but very enjoyable deviation.

Ballycroy National Park was a real treat in terms of foliage by the roadside, flowers, trees and wildlife in the forms of badgers, rabbits, squirrels, a total of five foxes and numerous varieties of birds. The chirping and songs of the latter emphasised the stillness and quietness of the woods. I loved it but was soon through it and into Bangor where I treated myself to fish and chips while I pondered over the decision of whether or not to reach the north coast by a direct route or to go via the road to Be mullet. A Garda patrol officer told me that it was about 50 miles to where I had planned to reach that night, namely Belderrig. One factor was in my favour and that was the strong wind from the south which had helped me enormously, especially on the hills.

The road along to Bunnahowen was quiet, twisty but fairly smooth. After a short distance I turned east up to Barnatra then back on the main road short of Glenamoy. About there the forest ended. Next I circled the peninsula via Porturlin. There I was so tired and worn out that I seriously considered setting up camp in a field close to the river but I kept going and on arrival in Belderrig booked into the 'Yellow Rose' B&B which was the first one I came to. Although rather late in the evening I was welcomed by Eileen and Stephen McHale, the proprietors, as if it was early evening. They also had a campsite but I was far too tired to bother with putting up the tent. Steven, Eileen and their daughter Rosie were eager for me to tell them all about my journey but firstly put me up a great plate of delicious, wholesome sandwiches with my usual suppertime drink of hot water but in this instance it was liberally dosed, with my consent, by Poitín and honey. What a nightcap!

I didn't wake up till almost 10am which was the latest I had slept so far but I felt so refreshed. There was a full view of the Atlantic from my window. I really didn't feel like rushing too much and certainly felt that I had cycled just a bit too far the previous day. I wouldn't do that in future because after all I was not subject to any form of timetable and was, so far, enjoying my experience. However, I realised that the excitement of completing the trip was beginning to influence my decisions about how far I would cycle each day even though the daylight hours were now longer than when I set off in April.

After breakfast Steven acquainted me with some local items of present day interest such as the long running dispute with Shell over their plans to start offshore drilling for oil to which the local fishermen objected. He also showed me the latest invention being brought into use by the fishermen in their boats. Basically it was a type of waterborne sail which prevented the boats rising up too high in the water whilst they were laying their nets. It was an ingenious idea and he said it worked perfectly. My contribution to the morning's conversation was to introduce them to the practice of dowsing. It really caught on with them all including the young woman who was their daily help. My final contribution involved giving them a demonstration of mediumship which went down very well. Finally, before I left Steven and Eileen presented me with a bottle of Poitín to 'help me on my way' they said. I looked forward to sampling it in the days and possibly even the weeks ahead but after my last few experiences of Poitín I would certainly not overdo it.

A short ride got me to Ballycastle where I stopped at a picnic site by the road to have a snack. A man, who said he was out for a walk, stopped for a chat. He was Michael DI Cerbo, an artist from the USA who during the summer months here, not only demonstrates his work at a local art gallery but also teaches art. He said he specialises in etchings and sells a whole range of his work on the Internet where anyone, by entering his name into Google can view it. Michael suggested I have a look at Downpatrick Head on my way to Ballycastle. He said it was famous for a 'sea stack' which was a gigantic rock formation close to the cliffs which looked like a pile of giant sandwiches. However, when I got to a point on the road nearest to it there was no way for me to take my bike across the fields. I didn't want to leave it by the roadside so I carried on down through Carrowmore and into Killala where I stopped at 'McDonalds Stop And Shop' to enquire about local overnight accommodation as time was wearing on. I wasn't going to repeat the previous night's experience of leaving it too late.

I spoke to a man in a car outside the shop who said he was waiting to collect his wife who worked there. At that moment his wife came out and got in the car. I enquired from them about B&Bs locally. The man, called Ted Cox, explained to his wife Marian what I was doing and that I was looking for a local campsite for the night. Their decision was unanimous. I was invited to be their guest for the night at their home in nearby Carrowsteel, Kilcummen. I agreed after stating that I would only accept their offer if I could pay the proper B&B rate. Ted said he would go home, drop Marian off and return with his van to collect me and the bicycle. To save Ted the bother of going for the van I said I would cycle to their place but he wouldn't hear of it. While they were gone I bought some wine and other things from the shop to take with me to their place. Soon he was back with his van and taken to their house on a hill overlooking Killala Bay. On the way he told me about one of the two dogs they had. He said it didn't take kindly to strangers so they had taken the precaution of putting it in the kennel with their other two dogs. When we got to his place and got my bike and panniers accommodated we went to where the two dogs were in a large kennel. I talked quietly to them and soon their tales were wagging in a friendly manner. I told Ted of my experience at Portaferry with a dog which had a similar reputation and persuaded him to let them out into the yard. After I had given them each a piece of chocolate neither one seemed to be too bothered about me. In fact the 'cross' one kept close to me all evening.

While Maria was making the evening meal Ted took me out in the car to show me all the beauty spots and historic sites but especially the amazing panoramic views out over Killala Bay, Sligo Bay and Donegal Bay. All of this they could view from their house. What a marvellous location. Maria served up a meal that would have equalled any meal in a top class hotel and afterwards we had a great evening of conversation and Irish music followed by supper. After being wined and dined in such style I went to my room well ready for sleep. The sun was shimmering on the still waters of the various bays the next morning when I awoke to the aroma of breakfast cooking. Whilst I ate and later improved my relationship with the three dogs by giving them various titbits, Ted took Maria to work. On his return I had a tour around the farm then coffee and biscuits before he dropped me back outside the shop where we had first met. The hospitality which Ted and Maria had shown me was such that overnight I felt I had made a true friendship with a couple who would be my friends for the years ahead. All my attempts at making payment for my stay were thwarted by their determination to show me that they had enjoyed my company. I was truly sad on parting from them but felt sure our paths would definitely cross again.

My next stop was Ballina where I went to the one and only mobile phone shop in the town to get some advice and help with topping up my IPhone credit. Somehow it didn't seem as simple a procedure as when I did it in Belfast for the first time. Well, to say I was disappointed with the service would be an understatement. A young woman and an older man were the only staff. The man didn't understand the IPhone at all and said it was a useless thing. He allowed me to use their phone to call my daughter in England and get the details I needed and charged me £1 for the call. All the while the young woman was totally engrossed on the 'phone telling someone about the wonderful time she had had at some function she had attended the night before. At no time did she offer to help nor did the man ask her to help.

Following the incident when I fell into the hedge at the roadside a few days previous I decided that I should get another helmet. The first one I had was one I had acquired in England a few years previous and was in fact a helmet as used by skateboarders. This was pointed out to me for the first time by some youths skateboarding on the promenade in Newcastle, county Down shortly after I had set out on this journey. Near Wexford I decided to dispense with it and in a moment of silliness left it on a farm gatepost with a note attached which said stated that I had brought it with me from outer space but now I didn't need it anymore! In 'Hopkins Cycles' Pearse Street, Ballina, I got kitted out with a cycle helmet and shown how to wear it properly by the very efficient young man running the place. Of course it was very careless of me not to have made sure I had the appropriate helmet before I came on this cycle trip. My only excuse is that I had been cycling all of sixty years without having felt the need for one. My experience, and lucky escape from serious injury involving the farm vehicles, was the first time in over sixty years of cycling that I had ever seriously thought about the value of wearing a cycle helmet.

Now, complete with new helmet I rode north through Crockets Town then took a narrow road along the River Moy up to Inishcrone where it became Killala Bay. At a number of points along the road up to Rathlee I was able to see Ted and Maria's house across the bay on Kilcummen Head. As I turned eastwards towards Esky their place was now behind me. I felt more than a little sad at the thought. At Esky I was joined for a short while by the young man called Jerry, from Dublin. He was making for a hostel in Sligo town that night. I got details of its whereabouts and hoped to meet up with him there that night.   For the rest of the afternoon my view to the north was dominated by Sligo Bay and again a host of islands big and small. All of this was added to by the number and variety of boats, large and small out in the bay but the best view of the bay was in the area of Templeboy where the road was quite close to the sea. There I stopped for a rest and snack on a high grassy bank with a good view out over the bay and also inland to the Ox Mountains. Two quite professional young cyclists called Eamonn and Noleen who were on a one week cycling tour from Derry joined me. We shared some chocolates and biscuits and tea from my flask and I took a few photographs of them posing with the bay behind them. We set off together but within minutes they were out of sight whilst I plodded along steadily. One pleasure I really enjoyed was stopping at good viewpoints to view the scenery through my binoculars. No way would I want to be without them. At a village called Rathlee I saw sculpture of a pig by the roadside. It was the size of a cow almost but I couldn't see any plaque on or near it to explain its significance, neither was there anyone about to ask.

It was getting dusk as I came to the Sligo International Tourist Hostel near the centre of the town and met up with Jerry there. He was sharing a three bed room with a very wild eyed middle aged man who struck me as either someone with a mental problem or on drugs but certainly I had no intention of sharing that room with him. I told the manager so and he allocated me a two bed room on the second floor and said I could have sole use of it as he didn't have a lot of bookings for that night. As I was arriving at the hostel I saw a big supermarket which was still open so after I got my accommodation arranged at the hostel I went there and did some shopping for some things for supper and breakfast. As it was near closing time I had my choice of a lot of bargains in the food section. Amongst the good few bargains I selected were two roast chickens for the price of one plus a carrier bag almost full of freshly cooked chicken thighs which, back home, would have lasted me for a week. I intended having one of the chickens for supper and the other for breakfast. As I left the supermarket I gave the bag of chicken thighs to a man in the street selling the magazines 'Big Issue'. At the hostel it was chicken supper then to bed.

In the morning when I went to the kitchen area to make my breakfast I was appalled to find the room in a mess. The cushions from a settee were thrown on the floor; there were numerous coins scattered everywhere; unwashed dishes were not only on the sink but on chairs; partly eaten sandwiches were scattered about the room and most of the cupboard doors were open. Several empty beer cans were also scattered about. I went and spoke with the manager who apologised for the state of the place. He explained that a young woman staying there had brought a man back from the pub which was against the hostel's rules. He first became aware of it when the couple, both of whom were drunk, started fighting and arguing in the kitchen about 2am. He had ejected both of them but hadn't as yet got around to tidying up the kitchen. I made myself a pot of tea and took it back to my room where I ate my chicken. I didn't see Jerry as I left but as the room he was in was next to the kitchen I don't think he would have had much sleep. I felt that I had been lucky in my choice of rooms. Earlier on my trip I had been given some advice about choosing hostels. It was advised that generally if I wanted peace and quiet I should avoid those in or near town centres where the clientele were more likely to be the rowdy variety and often locals with no homes. Those in out-of-town locations were frequented more by genuine travellers in cars, on motor cycles and others like me, on cycles. It now seemed to have been very appropriate advice.

The sound of planes going to and from Sligo airport added to the noise of the busy early morning traffic as I cycled towards Bundoran. It tempted me to take a deviation eastwards to Lough Gill, the setting for William Butler Yeats well known poem, 'The Lake Isle Of Innisfree' but like so many other places along the way such a visit would have to wait for another time. I had only gone a few miles when I had another roadside 'find', again on the grass verge. It was a perfectly clean looking tea towel which I knew would come in useful for purposes other than what it was intended. . My list of useful roadside 'finds' was definitely growing.

At Drumcliff I could see a heavy shower approaching over Mount Benbulbin and stopped in a gateway to a field to put on my waterproofs in readiness. As I was doing this my attention was drawn to a most peculiar sight about 200 yards away across the field. What I could see was something black, a few inches thick and about a foot long rising slowly from the ground then dropping back equally slowly. I watched this for a few minutes and was so intrigued that I decided to go and see what it was. I discovered that it was a ewe which was lying on its back in a hollow and couldn't get up because of all its wool. Its lamb, in a distressed state, was beside its mother. The poor ewe had obviously been there perhaps since last night as the ground around its head was all disturbed with the thrashing of its horns. I immediately lifted the ewe onto its feet but it was so weak it was unable, at first, to stand. Eventually however, it staggered off towards other sheep in the adjacent field once the lamb had managed to get a drink of milk. On a nearby fence four crows were obviously disappointed at losing the opportunity to attack the ewe's eyes once it had become unable to move. In the circumstances I was so elated at having saved the ewe from imminent misery and possibly death.

A little way further along the same road I came to the cemetery where Percy French is buried. Amongst the many well-known songs he composed is 'The Mountains of Mourne' and of course 'The Emigrants Letter'.   From Drumcliff I headed west on a minor road via Ballyconnell then back to the N15 at Grange. I didn't see much of the sea except at those two towns. What I found peculiar was that practically all the mountain tops in the Dartry range were flat topped at about the same height. I assumed that stemmed from when they were at some time in the ancient past, under the ocean. I came to the Town of Money Gold opposite Inishmurray Island. I asked a total of five local people I met as to the history behind the name but not one could help me. Later I 'phoned the Leitrim Champion Newspaper but they didn't know either. I also asked them about the significance of the big bronze pig I had seen on the previous day but nobody knew anything about it. They did refer me to a well-known local historian and gave me his telephone number but there was no reply to a number of my calls.

Next came the town of Bundoran which is reputed to be one of the most popular holiday resorts for the people of Ireland with its direct railway links both to Dublin and Belfast. On the way there I saw lots of empty and dilapidated holiday cottages which should not have been the case in the height of the tourist season. I found the town had a very pleasant beach but there were not many people about. I stopped at a cafe on the seafront and treated myself to a massive fish and chips meal whilst sitting outside in the sun. I was offered the local newspaper to read while I waited. I appreciated that little bit of local customer care and attention from the staff. In it I noticed several 'For Sale' adverts for holiday cottages, no doubt a sign of the times when people don't have a lot of money to spend on holidays either in Ireland or elsewhere. Ballyshannon, my next port of call was by contrast, bustling with locals and tourists. In a shop window I read all about the town's history which went back to the Neolithic period, 4000 – 2500 BC plus all about the ancient ruins unearthed locally and of skeletons being found with precious stones which had been placed in their hands. Here was a place that a person could explore for several weeks. I crossed the River Erne bridge and enjoyed the help I got from the back wind that took me past Doonin Point and St. John's Point towards my target for the evening, namely Donegal town. I had a quick look in the Tourist Information Centre in Donegal and collected some more information leaflets. Riding westwards past Mountcharles, Inver and Bruckles I had a superb view back across the bay from where I had just come. This is one attraction of travelling along a coastline where peninsulas are so common, especially if you keep to the roads nearest the coast because you can view the peninsulas from both sides as I have been doing.

At Straleeny I left the main road and in no time came into Killybegs. From a few enquiries I learnt that there was a very good hostel a few miles further on so as it was now late evening I carried on along that road and arrived at the Donegal Town Independent Hostel. The manageress, Linda, made me welcome and introduced me to several of the other guests, which I thought was a very considerate thing to do. It made me feel like I was one of a large family. I found the place in immaculate condition and quite full of guests from most of the continents. The diversity of languages in that kitchen was truly amazing but more amazing was the fact that most of them had a reasonable knowledge of English. I have a fair good knowledge of Spanish and that helped a lot, particularly with one couple from South America. They were from the Chile. Their names were Maria and Andreas. As I have a married son who lives in Chile we had a lot to talk about over our evening meal, which in fact she cooked for me along with their meal. As this was their first visit to Ireland they had a lot of questions for me. The fact that I could speak Spanish reasonably well meant a lot to them. They asked that when I next went to Chile I was to look them up. I had planned to be on the road for shortly after 6 am but couldn't because my bike was locked up overnight in a workshop at the back of the hostel and the key wasn't where Linda had said it would be. I didn't feel like disturbing Linda and her husband Andy so early as they were such a nice helpful couple the previous evening. Linda had told me where the workshop key would be but I couldn't find it. A couple of hours later it was Linda's husband who showed me where it was. It was where Linda had said it would be but I hadn't looked for it properly. It only meant that while I waited I drank a lot more coffee than I would have done and ate my way through a stack of pancakes, laden with marmalade that I shouldn't have done and chatted to a good few of the other guests. Linda took a lot of interest in my cycling adventure. She asked that I let her know when I had completed the journey.

At a specially laid out roadside view point a short distance beyond the village of Largy I stopped to have my last view of Donegal Bay before the road would take me inland and then northwards along the west coast. Three young French women who were at the Killybegs hostel arrived in their car. They were all fun and laughter at the hostel and were the same here. With their cameras I took various photographs of them with the bay in the background and of course with me included then they were off again, still laughing, excited and thoroughly enjoying themselves leaving my face covered in lipstick and a big box of biscuits on my bike. While I was involved with them three cars, laden with Asian men and women arrived and very quickly also began taking photographs. They too were all very jolly and when I asked if they would like me to take their photographs for them they readily agreed.

I was in the midst of doing this when my brother Martin and his wife Irene arrived in their car. It was a fantastic surprise for me. The previous evening I had a routine phone call from their daughter Teresa and during the conversation I told her where I was staying in Killybegs. What I didn't realise was that the mum and dad were planning to give me a surprise visit the very next day. In the midst of my welcoming Martin and Irene, the Asians left after thanking me profusely but I didn't get any kisses from their women. The three French girls had left lots of lipstick all over my cheeks. Maybe that was why the Asian ladies didn't give me any kisses!

Well, that was the end of my trip for that day and very nearly the end of it altogether if Martin and Irene had their way! In no time my bike was in their car and we were off along the coast, stopping here and there but eventually ending up in Ardara where we all booked into Brae House B&B. We had a big evening meal, then to a local pub where there was Irish music and singing. The place was packed and we were there until the small hours of the following morning. The three of us had a great night. It meant so much to me to see them. I was teasing Martin that he didn't believe that this old codger of a brother was actually cycling the whole way around the coast of Ireland and had come to check up on me.

The hostess, Mrs Nora Molloy made a very late breakfast for us. I expected that Martin and Irene would then be off back to County Down but they had other plans, namely that I pack in this nonsense business of cycling around Ireland and go back across to their place for a holiday before returning to England. Martin said I looked 'all done in and haggard' but I said that was due to them keeping me up all night. They tried hard to persuade me to go home with them. I certainly felt in no fit state to do any cycling that day but no way was I being persuaded to abandon my trip, especially now that I was over half way around the country. But I came up with a compromise. It was that they drive me all the way along the rest of my route back to the Giant's Causeway where they could leave me at a hostel and go on home. By then I would have recovered sufficiently to be able to cycle back along the same coast road and complete my journey where they had met me instead of at the Giant's Causeway. That seemed to convince them that I really was a glutton for punishment, but they agreed to my plan and off we went.

In Dunglow we stopped for a break and Irene bought three lottery tickets and gave one each to Martin and I. When I checked mine I found I had won fifty Euros. Later I put it towards the cost of petrol for the car.

Having spent one and a half months travelling at an average speed of about fifteen miles per hour it was now quite a change to be travelling at twice that speed in the car but it seemed as if we were travelling at 100 mph!. The effect of it really did take some getting used to as we followed the main road up to the north of Donegal then down again through Derry and finally arrived at a youth hostel at Ballintoy on the North Antrim coast that evening. There I said goodbye to Martin and Irene as they set off to Mourne and I booked into the Whitepark Bay Youth Hostel on the shore of Rathlin Sound. The sight of Rathlin Island took my mind back to that first day on the road and the first time I had seen the island. The lady in charge gave me a room overlooking the sea. From my bedroom window that night I could see a lighthouse flashing on Rathlin Island. I could also see a line of about a dozen small lights moving out to sea in a northerly direction and guessed that they were fishing boats. In special locations such as this I always like to listen to night time sounds as I drift off to sleep but there was nothing but absolute silence which was a most unusual experience.

The following morning it was a rather strange feeling to have the sea on my right hand side instead of it being on my left. I experienced a mixture of feelings as I passed the entrance to the Giant's Causeway where I had begun this trip. I certainly hadn't ever imagined being here other than at the end of it all. By lunchtime I was making my way along a road close to the coast of Lough Foyle when I saw a sign outside a house advertising pots of jam for sale. The house name was 'Annaclone'. On a chair by the front door there were pots of jam of various sizes, each labelled with its price. The chair was covered with a pretty white cloth which had on it a dish with lots of change in it and a sign which said, 'Help yourself". There was nobody about but I rang the doorbell and while I waited for someone to come out I photographed the chair and its contents. The thought in my mind at that time was how trusting the occupants must be to do this. I could think of so many places where passers-by would indeed help themselves to the jam, and the money! A man came to the door and apologised for the delay. He said he had been working in the back garden with his wife and that people didn't normally ring the bell. They just took the jam and left the money. I explained that I was a stranger and was particularly surprised to see their display of faith in people's honesty. He was in the process of telling me how, in the years they had been doing this, nobody had taken jam without paying for it when his wife joined us. He said she was the jam maker. After I had introduced myself I learned that they were Roberta and Clement McCartney and that they had lived there for the past five years but that she had been making jam all her life. I asked her where she was from as her accent obviously wasn't Irish. She explained that she was from Chile. I couldn't believe this. In two days I had met people from Chile! I told her about my son living in Chile and in the conversation that followed she was from a town quite near to where he lives. Well, we were all flabbergasted at the coincidence involved in our meeting in these circumstances. At their garden table in brilliant sunshine we had coffee and a special home-made cake which Roberta had made and talked for almost an hour. After a session of photographs I bought two small pots of jam and had to insist that I pay for them. It was only after all this time that I learned from them that they were then almost an hour late for an appointment at the doctors' surgery. They wanted me to wait until they came back so that we could have lunch together but I declined explaining that I wanted to get the ferry at Magilligan Point as soon as possible. How refreshing it always is to meet such nice people!

Along the road on my way to the ferry I my next 'find'. It was a white baseball type cap in good condition. It was the type with a sun flap at the back which was just what I needed to keep the sun off my neck. I had to wait for a while on the ferry so I took that opportunity to wash the cap in the toilets and dry it under the hand dryer. By the time the ferry was ready I had cut the peak off the cap also the adjusting strap at the back so that the cap would fit perfectly under my cycle helmet leaving the flap clear at the back. When I came off the ferry I followed signs to Ballintroohan on the coast but that road took me south again to Lockemy before I was able to head westwards on the very long, hard ride up towards Malin Head to a hostel which I had seen advertised in one of the brochures. The road to Malin Head took me through real mountainous country but I didn't mind that so much as the wind was once again behind me. This was a fairly rugged coastline with few houses and small farms and not many animals in the fields but after all this was the most northerly point of Ireland. At Malin Head it took some effort to find the 'Sandrock Holiday Hostel'. It wasn't signposted anywhere but locals did help with directions. People kept referring me to 'the cross' when they meant crossroads which really baffled me as I couldn't see any cross or anything like a cross in the direction which they sent me. I eventually found the hostel through the help of a young girl on a bike who rode with me to the end of the driveway leading to it. Rodney and Margaret, the proprietors, welcomed me and even let me select a room from the last three available. Every facility that anyone would want was there including Wi-Fi. The kitchen was spacious and again had every category of cooking equipment that would be the envy of many a hotel chef. The surroundings were like some place specially chosen for a film. I had arrived just before dusk but nevertheless I went for a walk away along the beach to sample the atmosphere of this most magical setting. The waters of Trawbreaga Bay washed up on a sandy beach not fifty yards from the hostel. Seabirds of every description were not only in the air but foraging amongst the lichen covered stones further up the beach. The hostel nestled underneath a big hill set out in fields where cows and calves called to each other likewise sheep and their lambs. Somewhere up on that hill a couple of corncrakes were busy calling to each other while beside me a few small fishing boats bobbed up and down on the water next to the tiny harbour called Port Ronan. I saw the lights come on in houses away across the bay casting their reflections on the calm water like long white fingers reaching out towards a little island in the middle of the bay. Bats zoomed past me everywhere and waves lapped up on the rocks. I had never experienced this atmosphere anywhere I had been. I sat for over an hour simply revelling in it all before making my way back to the hostel, supper and bed. I left the bedroom window open to let the sound of the waves and the calling of the birds lull me into sleeping in. In the morning I went to the little harbour beside the hostel and from the vantage point of its wall I scanned the bay for any sign of the dolphins and sharks which frequent its waters. Every year, for the purposes of research into shark migration all over the world, a huge number of them are caught in the bay, tagged and then released. I didn't see any. Next I went along the beach right under the sandstone cliffs to see the array of pebbles of every colour, size and shape which Rodney had told me about. I was fascinated by them and had a great problem selecting three to take away as souvenirs. He told me about a lady who had come on holiday from abroad many years ago and on seeing these stones had set up a very successful Donegal business called 'Malin Pebbles' from which she sells the stones worldwide on the Internet. He also told me that it was from Malin Head that the first transatlantic wireless message was transmitted by Marconi. It was mid-morning before I could wrest myself away from Malin Head and set off southwards on the Inishowen Peninsula. I had planned to take a shortcut by ferry across Lough Swilly from Buncrana to Rathmullen but found that it wasn't starting its summer season until the following day. If I had known this sooner I would have stayed an extra day at the the hostel in Malin Head. However, I rode on via the little town on Dunaff which eventually brought me to the very much busier town of Buncrana. A few miles south of there, with sandwiches made from soda bread and fruit bought in Buncrana I had a picnic on the beach where the island of Inch seemed just a stones throw away across the inlet. Helped enormously by a strong northerly wind I covered a lot of miles in what seemed a short time. I concentrated on the task of cycling and soon I passed through the outskirts of Derry then across the Swilley River to Letterkenny. Enquiries I made for accommodation took me to no less than five B&Bs all of which were full due to a very big car rally taking place that week covering the whole of that area of

Donegal. Eventually I came to the Mountain View B&B in Churchill, where one room was available. The rest had already been booked by some of the car rallying fraternity. It had been a long ride so as soon as I had a meal I was into bed.

Very heavy rain delayed my setting off the next morning until nearly 10am when, with warning about the rally traffic from Susan and Tony at the B&B, I was back on the bike. I stuck with narrow country roads across to Rathmullan then northwards hoping to make it to Fanad Head area by lunchtime but the going was hard. There was indeed a lot of traffic on all the roads and I recognised the familiar set up of rally cars but they didn't cause me any problems. Mid-afternoon saw me in Fanad Head which is dominated by its white lighthouse on the cliff top with wild Atlantic waves lashing the cliffs below it. Like Malin head here was an area which would take at least a week to enjoy its scenery and learn of its history. I spent a mere half an hour having a quick ride around the town. I saw a pub called 'The Claddagh Bar' so I just had to have a drink there as I was the proud wearer of a Claddagh ring. In the bar I met Eamon Clinton, a man who I had first met on a campsite in Torre Del Mar, in Spain, some years previously, which led to me having more than just one drink. Feeling invigorated with the few beers I had, Kindrum soon came and went as I took a wide westward loop around a big sea inlet then down the main road to Milford. Now it was up to Carrickart with nothing but mountains on my left and a narrow strip of lough on my right then south along the shore of Sheep Haven bay.

Next was the town of Creeslough, made famous by Percy French's Irish ballad called 'The Emigrant's Letter' but made truly famous by the singer Bridie Gallagher in the 1970s.

By the time I reached Dunfanaghy I was worn out and well ready for the excellent accommodation at the hostel of the same name. It was a quick supper there and then bed. Next morning just after daybreak I slipped quietly out of the hostel and set off southwards as the sun was rising. I deliberately set off early as I intended to make it back to Killybegs and thus complete my circuit of Ireland, albeit not all in a clockwise direction as I had originally intended. In Gortahork and Knockfold people were just getting up and the countryside was coming to life as it were when I passed through. Out over the big rolling Atlantic waves there were spectacular views of Inishbofin Islands and away in the distance Tory Island, both of which are well known locations in both Irish history and folklore. In a school gateway I stopped to adjust my gears and spoke to a two cleaners going in to work there. I asked if they could tell me the history behind the unusual name of the nearby Bloody Foreland. They told me that if I came back in the evening when the sun is setting the rocks on the foreland would all take on a reddish appearance of blood, hence the name. The second lady said that there was also a legend that a nasty giant had been slain there by the fairies and his blood had spread over the rocks giving them that red colour in the evenings. Now that sounded more like what I would have expected the reason to be!

Near Derrybeg I had a quick breakfast at a small cafe next to a garage and kept going. It was a really beautiful sunny morning. With The Rosses rising ahead of me, the Derryveagh Mountains on my left and a host of islands out to sea on my right I was spoilt for choice as to my choice of scenery. The ideal cycling conditions which appertained when I had set out that morning still persisted. I was really enjoying this day, which was to be the last day of my tour. The road hugged the coast most of the way down to Maas where I took a side road at Naran which in turn took me away from the coast through farmland, with very few houses, then back to the main road again. On the way I saw a dead lamb on the grass verge. It was my guess that it had been hit by a vehicle during the night or earlier that morning. Its mother was bleating loudly behind the hedge through which it had obviously escaped from the field. Two large rats were already hard at work on the remains of the poor creature. I got off my bike, chased the rats then took the lamb a short distance to the gateway and put it over to the care of its mother. It was a sad sight to behold as the mother licked away its blood hoping obviously to revive it. It put me in a sombre mood until I reached Ardara where I had stayed overnight with Martin and Irene.

Now that I was at last within reach of Killybegs I stopped for a late lunch at a cafe in the main street in Adara followed by a few cool beers instead of the usual tea or coffee. It was almost teatime when I began what was to be the last leg of the journey via Glencolumbkille then back to where I met Martin and Irene. This route was through mountains with steep climbs but equally many long downhill stretches which made up for the time lost on cycling up the hills but my legs were beginning to feel the strain which I blamed that on the few beers I had earlier. When I reached Glencolumbkille that was to be the last west facing road on which I would travel. With a tinge of sadness that my exciting trip was nearing its end I made my way with both the sun and the breeze from the Atlantic behind me past Slieve League where the road runs between the big and the small lakes and finally Kilcar to the roadside picnic site where I met Martin and Irene. I stopped, had a coffee from my flask, finished off the last lot of sandwiches and my dwindling store of chocolates.

At the Donegal Independent Youth Hostel Linda was so surprised to see me back there having told her less than a week previous I told her that I was on my way up the west coast and back to Northern Ireland. I tried to kid her on that I had completed my clockwise trip and was now doing the anticlockwise version of it but she was far too smart to swallow that one. I finally explained about meeting up with Martin and Irene and all that followed. She congratulated me on what I had achieved. She gave me the impression that she truly meant every word she spoke. It meant a lot to me as she was the first person I had spoken to since I had completed my task just a few miles away. I will admit I felt quite emotional about it and no doubt showed signs of my feelings because she gave me a big hug and said, "Patrick, I feel quite honoured that you have come here straight from the end of your ride. You can have your old room if you

like. You know where it is. I must go and tell Andy". He
came through from their house, shook my hand and also
congratulated me. I began to feel a little bit like some
sort of celebrity. But then came the bad news! When I
explained that in the morning I was going into the town
to get a train to Belfast she laughed and said, "You'll be
lucky. There is no railway station in Donegal Town you
know". I thought she was joking but she wasn't. I
couldn't believe that a big town like Donegal didn't have
a railway station. Linda, as helpful as ever, told me not
to worry as she could put me in touch with a good car
hire company locally and if I wanted I could resolve my
problem that way. "I'll have it sorted for you by the
morning", she said, "Don't you worry about it tonight".

I went into the lounge to make myself a drink. A young
man was there poring over a map of Ireland and of
course we began a conversation in which I learnt that his
name was Albert and he was from the Netherlands. He
explained that he had come for one week to do a coastal
circuit of Ireland and that the following morning he was
setting off to see the west coast and as much of the
northern coast as he could then the following evening be
back in Dublin. He went on to say that he was trying his
best to understand the printed English language in the
various brochures and on the maps. Well, I could hardly
believe what I was hearing. Here was a lone man in a
car going tomorrow to Northern Ireland where I wanted
to go. I could hardly wait to tell him of my predicament
and see if there was any possibility that I could
accompany him. Immediately he seemed so relieved and
asked there and then if I would be his guide along his

route. I looked at his map and the marks showing where he wanted to stop and take photographs. I had been to every one of those places within the past few days. We shook hands but felt before things went any further we would have to check if my bike would fit in his car.

At first he didn't think it would but when I said explained I would remove both wheels we agreed that the bike and panniers and his luggage would all fit in the car. He seemed as happy as I was. I had to smile when he said in his serious way of speaking, "I am so pleased that you will be my native Irish guide in your country". I felt a bit like one of those native Indian guides in some sort of Western film. Needless to say I immediately thanked Linda for her offer of help and the next morning Albert and I were on our way. What he wanted to do most of all was to visit various locations on the coast which were featured in his tour guide. With his book and map I became his official 'native Irish guide'.

As we set off Albert explained that whilst he had a Driving Licence for a car and a motor cycle he rarely drove a car. I didn't worry about all that too much. After all he had driven this far after arriving in Dublin without mishap. His main worry seemed to be that of 'driving on the wrong side of the road' from what he was familiar with back home. As the morning wore on I could see that not only was he driving too fast most of the time but he was driving the car as if it was a motorbike. Even his posture behind the wheel indicated that. Definitely he was handling the car on corners as if it was a motor bike. To put it mildly, within a few miles I was having fears for my safety. Nevertheless, I was going to keep quiet about any opinions I had on his driving because I was so grateful for this opportunity to get back to Belfast. I took him to more locations than I had visited so that he could take photographs of places of interest but particularly beauty spots. Always it was a case of stopping, taking photographs then racing to the next destination. In comparison with the speed to which I had become accustomed to on my bike this experience was definitely like being in a jet plane. My previous car journey over almost the same route and in the same direction over a week previous with Martin and Irene gave me the same sensation but not to the same degree as this was doing. This was definitely scary.

That first night we stayed at the hostel in Dunfanaghy where I had stayed earlier in the week and the next day completed the route to the Giant's Causeway where we both had a final session of taking photographs. That evening I found him a hostel in the centre of Belfast as he had wished for but when he saw the protective grilles around pub doorways and various other indications of this troubled city he wanted to go elsewhere. As his trusted 'native guide' I was able to reassure him that he would not come to any harm. I felt he didn't believe me so I took him to one such pub, almost next door to his hostel and introduced him to the three tough looking guards behind their grille and explained his fears to them. They shook hands with him and invited him to come back later after he had got settled into his room and they would ensure he had a good time. They assured me that one of them would even escort him back to the hostel door. Albert seemed happy with that but I doubted if he would venture out of the hostel before the morning.

I stayed overnight at a hotel on the outskirts of Belfast from where Moira collected me the following morning and took me to the airport. I had the bike all prepared for the flight and everything went smoothly until I got to the Airport Security checkpoint. There the very special miniature set of cycle tools, worth about £35, which I had been lent by Michael Myers back at Inch was confiscated because one of the tools, about two inches long, had a screwdriver point. No amount of protesting on my part could reverse the decision by the rather young man on the checkpoint who didn't know it was a set of cycle tools until I told him. Not even the intervention of Moira, who said she would take it and send it to me in the UK, could reverse the officer's decision. As I was the last passenger to board the plane I had to abandon my protest and literally ran to the waiting plane staff.

On my arrival at Robin Hood Airport I had the same experience with my bike as I had on my arrival at Belfast Airport, namely a buckled rear wheel due to the carelessness of the either the staff at Belfast Airport or at Robin Hood Airport. However, I once again undid the rear brake system and managed to cycle home on it. If ever I make such an aeroplane trip again with a cycle I'll make sure to remove both front and rear wheels and put my cycle tools with the cycle. However I didn't let either of those unhappy events spoil my overall enjoyment of a wonderful experience which will last me a lifetime.

Written during September 2010 with assistance of notes, tape recordings, photographs, various documents and, of course, personal memories.

See Updates at:

http://www.AroundIrelandClockWiseOnAGiant.com

Made in the USA
Charleston, SC
25 April 2011